Scottish Offpiste Skiing & Snowboarding

Glencoe

A Guide to Skiing & Snowboarding Offpiste, Steep Skiing, and Ski Mountaineering
by Kenny Biggin

Photos & Diagrams by Kenny Biggin except where stated.
Entry diagrams by Ali Martin: www.westcoastart.co.uk
Design and layout by lamontdesign: www.lamontdesign.co.uk
SkiMountain logo design by www.crofteleven.co.uk

Cover Images:
Front: Dragon Bowl, Creise. Rider: Neil Muir
Back Top: Stob Ghabhar, Riders: Brian Morrison & Kev Quinn
Back Left: Creag Dhubh Chute. Rider: Kenny Biggin
Back Middle: Skyfall Bowl. Rider: John Sutherland
Back Right: Monument Glencoe. Rider: Andy Meldrum

1st Edition by Kenny Biggin 2014
Published by SkiMountain Ltd
www.SkiMountain.co.uk
 /SkiMountain.co.uk

ISBN 978-0-9926065-1-0
A catalogue record is available from the British Library

MIX
Paper from responsible sources
FSC® C023105
FSC www.fsc.org

Acknowledgements

Firstly thanks to all of you who bought the first book – the guide to Nevis Range & Ben Nevis – which has made it possible to produce this one. Big thanks go to Ali Martin for turning my childlike sketches into the diagrams you see here, and for humouring me (again!) – these books would not have happened without her help and encouragement. Thanks to all my skiing buddies, and everyone who has shared photos and information about routes, conditions, history, and Glencoe arcana. Thanks to Philip Rankin (and all those who helped him) for having the foresight to think building a lift system on Meall a' Bhuiridh was a good idea – Scottish skiing as it exists today is a direct result of the pioneering work done by Philip and others all those years ago. And of course thanks to my parents for getting me into skiing in the first place, and for their proof reading services.

Some special mentions are deserved by: Doug Bryce who shared a wide variety of information; Ron Cameron who helped me steer through the minefield of Gaelic words; Scottish ski lift pioneer Jimmy Hamilton who kept me right on parts of the history section, and also gave permission for his piece on early skiing in Glencoe to be part of the book; any errors are mine, not theirs. Thanks also to the current owner of White Corries, Andy Meldrum, who is doing great things for the place; and to the Glencoe Mountain Resort staff and locals for making me welcome. Thanks also to the following: SAIS staff, Andy Nelson, Davy Gunn, Scott Muir, Nigel Wombell, Ken Marsden, Blair Fyffe, Graham Moss, Graham Pinkerton, Martin Burrows-Smith, Jamie Johnston, Stephen Speirs, Ed Smith, Kevin Quinn, Angela Anderson, David Shortt, Bobby and Jack Williamson, Mike Guest, Keith & Christine Hill, Billy Lamont, George Paton, Jordan Tiernan, Brian Morrison, Dave Biggin, John Sutherland, and Neil Muir. Apologies to those I've missed out. Thanks also to all of the book's sponsors.

Disclaimer

Offpiste skiing and boarding are inherently dangerous activities in an unpredictable environment. Routes can and do change dramatically depending on conditions. You must decide for yourself what you are and aren't capable of doing, and whether the conditions are favourable at any particular time. It is good practice to build a margin for error into your activities and allow for 'what-if' scenarios such as equipment failure, inaccurate information, avalanches, falls, and other dangers. You must also be aware of the impact your decisions can have on other mountain users and the dangers that you expose them to.

The information provided in this book has been given in good faith but accuracy of route descriptions, diagrams, photos, locations etc. can never be guaranteed. This book is just one of a number of different sources of information you should use to ensure safe and enjoyable outings. The author, publisher, and anyone else involved in the production of this book, can bear no liability for any injury or death resulting from pursuit of activities in this book. Ski and board safely – the responsibility is yours!

Preface

This time last year, I was sitting here writing a preface to the offpiste guidebook for a different area – Nevis Range and Ben Nevis – which lies around forty minutes to the North of Glencoe. However, although Nevis is now my home turf, my skiing story actually started a little earlier shortly before Nevis Range opened.

Back in the late 1980's, my sister Catherine and I were among many young kids whose parents dropped them off early in the morning at the West End car park in Fort William. Every day for most weekends through the season, as part of the West Highland Ski Club, we got on a coach which took us down to the ski lifts at Glencoe. We would arrive at the car park, often still in the dark, and walk up to where the original one man access chairlift started. I have a lasting memory of being a small, cold kid on that access chairlift, already soaked through my second hand cagoule in the rain, clutching my skis carefully across my lap while the rickety chairs swung alarmingly in the wind. At the top of the old access chair, there was another walk up to the bottom of the poma, or if there wasn't enough snow the walk was even longer across the plateau.

Eventually we would arrive at the ski club hut at the top of the Cliffhanger chair with just enough time to physically wring out our C&A gloves and fight over space beside the radiator before our ski lessons started. Despite being occasionally wet and cold, we must have been enjoying it because I also remember that we rarely stopped at lunchtime – instead opting to do laps jumping out of the Canyon, always squeezing one more run of 'free skiing' in whenever possible. This was a superb grounding in skiing for us, and a lot of good skiers came out of that group. The ethos continues today with scores of youngsters taking part in training every weekend with Glencoe Ski Club.

Little did I know back then that almost thirty years later I would be writing a book about the place. Although a few of the old lifts survive, there have been many improvements at Glencoe Mountain Resort since those days; and despite the fact that the weather still isn't great all the time, when the snow gods smile on us and the sun comes out this is a remarkable place to ski. As for the offpiste potential in the surrounding mountains… well, hopefully this book will give you a peek at the amazing skiing on offer here – take a look inside, pick a route, and go and find yourself an adventure. In the unbeatable words of Warren Miller who fuelled my generation of kids with his ski films:

"If you don't do it this year, you'll be one year older when you do!"

I couldn't have said it better myself.

Kenny Biggin, Spean Bridge. May 2014

We'll post any updates and new routes to you if you:
Like us on Facebook – /SkiMountain.co.uk

Contents

Stunning views over Loch Tulla

photo **Kenny Biggin**

Introduction

This is a guidebook to the amazing offpiste skiing and boarding possibilities in Glencoe. The book is centred around the ski lifts at Glencoe Mountain Resort (Meall a' Bhuiridh, also known as The White Corries) but includes many of the other great mountains that lie close by including Creise, Clach Leathad, the Buachailles, and the Bidean nam Bian massif, amongst others.

The book's area is roughly demarcated by the location of the A82 Glencoe snow gates which are closed when too much of the white stuff inundates the glen and makes driving impossible. The gates lie just North of Tyndrum, and just South of Glencoe village... although the highly deserved inclusion of Ben Lui and Beinn a' Bheithir on either side of this rather arbitrary boundary allows for skiing options even when the road is closed. The area was chosen in part because this is where one of the five main Scottish ski resorts is based, but more importantly because of the density of high mountains and good skiable terrain here within easy reach of one of Scotland's higher roads - for over twenty kilometres, the A82 stays above 250metres from the Meeting of Three Waters to the Black Mount.

The book not only provides route by route descriptions with as many good colour photos and illustrations as could be crammed in, but also includes chapters on the history, equipment, and safety required to get the most out of skiing and boarding in these mountains.

© SkiMountain

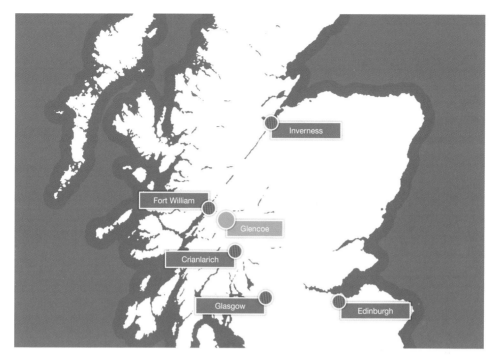

Although written by a skier, this book is aimed at all forms of snowsports including skiing, telemarking, snowboarding, and any others. Instead of trying to be politically correct the whole way through, the terms 'ski', 'skier' and 'skiing' have often been used generically to cover whatever the reader's chosen sport is. Please don't take offence to this as it makes the book much more readable than having to say 'skiers or boarders' every time.

Route Choice

The area covered could have easily encompassed almost thirty Munros, along with a multitude of lower summits. Amongst these hills there are a myriad of potential routes, with so many variations that it would be almost impossible to catalogue them all. With such a plethora of mountains and possibilities available, this book takes a pragmatic approach to route selection. The routes described here are a selection of high quality, classic routes, the majority of which will be possible for at least part of most seasons. No doubt other routes have been skied, and undoubtedly there are still other fantastic lines that have yet to see descents. It is hoped that this first edition provides a solid introduction to the offpiste on offer here, while laying a foundation for future exploration and adventure.

Without exception, every route included in this book has been skied at least once – the vast majority of them have been skied by the author and for the few that haven't, as close to a first hand account of the route as possible has been used.

A Note on Snow Cover

The majority of the research, photographs, and writing for this book was done during the winter of 2014, which (above a certain height) was the snowiest for a generation. Where possible, the unusual depth of snow has been taken into account when choosing and grading routes, but inevitably some of the descriptions may seem a little generous to those who attempt descents of the same routes in leaner seasons. The variation of route conditions from one season to the next (and indeed from one day to the next) is part and parcel of offpiste skiing, nowhere more so than in Scotland, and the reader needs to develop the ability to factor this into their decision making process. With luck, we will continue to see these depths of snow on a more regular basis for many years to come (down to around 300metres would be nice) and perhaps the cover seen in some of these photos will begin to look more commonplace rather than epic.

Left or Right?

Throughout the book it is common for route descriptions to talk about left and right directions. This can be extremely confusing because left when looking up the hill is of course right when coming down. To make the directions less ambiguous the terms left and right are usually accompanied by a qualifying word. When you see 'skier's left' or 'skier's right', it is referring to the direction from the skier's perspective (i.e. going downhill). When referring to directions from the point of view of looking up the hill, the terms used are usually 'looker's right', 'skinner's left', or 'climber's right'.

Naming

When it comes to naming routes for a new guidebook, there are bound to be a number of issues. Many of the bowls and corries in the area have existing Gaelic names, while most of the steeper gullies tend to have been named in climbing guidebooks decades (and in some cases over a century) ago. From a climbing point of view the skiable gullies and faces are usually either too easy to grade or will be Grade I or II winter routes. What's more these routes will often be used as descent routes and tend not to be given imaginative and inspiring names. Climbing names for such routes are all too often repetitive, for instance there are a large number of lines named Central Gully, Summit Gully, Broad Gully, Descent Gully, Gully Number 3, etc.

While it is of course important to preserve the sense of mountaineering history, and our Gaelic heritage, it is also seen as being important for the development of our sport for these routes to be given inspiring, entertaining, memorable, and where possible unique names. So while any existing known names are always mentioned for posterity within the route descriptions, in some cases where it is deemed appropriate routes have been given new names for use in a skiing context. No doubt this policy will be contentious with some, but over time it is hoped that people will appreciate the reasoning behind this approach.

There are also plenty of examples of routes that are known to different people by differing names. Inevitably, this guide will have failed to capture every single different route name ever thought up by skiers and that is unfortunate but unavoidable. It is hoped that those skiers affected will enjoy the names used and let the publisher know of such cases in order for future editions to be able to make amends. There is a small section at the back of the book aimed at helping out with pronunciation and translation of some of the more common Gaelic names.

Sharing & Responsibility

The decision to publish this book has not been taken lightly - will this book condemn secret powder stashes to being tracked out straight away? Will skiers be encouraged to ski unwittingly into danger? Will currently remote and peaceful bowls become full of freeriders and less wild? There is a big enough selection of routes and few enough Scottish skiers that it's hard to see that overcrowding will become a problem here... and if it did, perhaps it would pay for more lifts! It is also hoped that in placing route information alongside safety advice, skiers will become more aware of the hazards and increased participation will go hand in hand with improvements in awareness and good decision making.

Some local riders no doubt would prefer to keep Creise or the back of Glencoe to themselves, but it is hoped that one or two runs down such classics as The Big Easy on Clach Leathad, or Paradise on Bidean nam Bian will be enough to change their minds.

In writing this guidebook it is hoped that more people will be encouraged to enjoy and explore the amazing skiing offered by this area – in part because Glencoe Mountain Resort needs people to continue to ski here so that the operation remains sustainable. Along with its sister guidebook to Nevis Range & Ben Nevis, this book provides almost two hundred different alternatives so there should be plenty of room for everyone.

Route Descriptions and Grading

Skiing and boarding offpiste is by its nature a free and non-prescriptive activity and this fact has tried to be reflected when writing this guide. Although the descriptions are based around each different route, there are often many variations and the difficulty of a particular line can vary enormously depending what the conditions are like at the time.

Illustrated Panel

similar to:	Baillies
harder than:	Broad Gully
combine with:	Creag Dhubh Chute

An illustrated panel is provided to give you an overall impression of each route, which should allow you to make your own judgement calls about what you are ready to tackle and when. Comparisons are often made with other routes you may have skied already so that you can gradually work your way up and build an understanding of the routes which are appropriate for your ability as you go along. If you haven't skied much in this area before then you would be well advised to start off by skiing some of the easier sounding routes, or even the normal runs on the front of Glencoe Mountain. Good first routes for anyone new to offpiste skiing here are the East Ridge, the Fly Paper, and Baillies. Likewise, a good place to start skiing further afield is a trip across to Creise and back, or an easy tour away from the lifts up Buachaille Etive Beag or The Easy Eagach.

Difficulty Rating

All of the runs in this guidebook are offpiste backcountry routes – they all travel through avalanche terrain and all of them (even the easiest) can have hazards such as cornices, ice, rocks, or cruddy snow that can injure the unwary.

Until the publication of the sister book in this series (Scottish Offpiste - Nevis Range & Ben Nevis), there hadn't been a tradition in Scotland of either offpiste guidebooks or grading offpiste routes, so a decision had to be made about which, if any, existing system to adopt. Since the skiing in Scotland is uniquely... Scottish, and there were a variety of perceived problems with other grading systems from abroad, it seemed to make sense for a new grading system to be used. Most routes fall fairly easily into a small number of grades, so using 1 to 5 seems to work well.

The system often used in the Alps has grade subdivisions such as 3.2, 5.1, or 5.4. However, the system used here should not be confused with the Alpine one and has no subdivisions or direct relationship with it. This Scottish system assumes each difficulty rating covers a fairly wide spectrum and offers more of a strong hint about a particular route's difficulty rather than an extremely precise grading which is impossible in such an ever changing environment.

In the Nevis book there were a few routes that had been skied (often only once) that even in rare conditions are only just skiable. Rather than leave the 1-5 system open ended which in other sports tends to encourage 'grade hunting', that book bundled anything perceived to fall beyond the fifth grade into a single category labelled simply 'X' which means 'not graded'. In this edition of the Glencoe book, there aren't any routes which seemed to warrant this category although there is little doubt that there are several lines in the area which (if ever skied) would certainly fit under this umbrella.

The most important thing to keep reminding yourself when it comes to difficult or marginal routes is to ensure you are skiing them for the right reasons - ski them to test yourself, to commune with nature, to ski a dream line. Some things should be done for yourself and nobody else - would you still ski it if you knew nobody would ever know you'd skied it? Yes, at the upper grades they are all hard, and some will be harder than others - but which route is most difficult or most steep should become unimportant in comparison to the aesthetics of the line and its personal appeal to the skier.

Take pride in your ability to complete runs successfully, safely, in good style, in making good decisions and never having dangerous epics.

Scottish Offpiste Route Grades

Author's Note: All grades assume good conditions

1 These routes are the most accessible offpiste runs and in nice snow will be options even for intermediate skiers. There will not be any significant steepness to contend with and the runs will rarely be steeper than a red run. In some cases these routes will be accessed via a harder route or some ski touring.

- **Adrenaline Scale:** Fun and Not Steep
- **Example Routes:** The Access, Weasel Track, The East Ridge, Ba Cottage, Diamond Col

2 These routes start to provide an introduction to steeper offpiste skiing. The routes will largely be similar to black runs, but will often be steeper than this at the start. The routes will be open in nature and in good conditions falls will usually not be serious.

- **Adrenaline Scale:** Not too Steep
- **Example Routes:** Fly Paper, Lost Bowl, Baillies, Monument, Broad Gully

3 The skill level required for these routes begins to go up with short sections (usually at the entrance) starting to be quite steep.

- **Adrenaline Scale:** Quite Steep
- **Example Routes:** Local Hero, Skyfall Face, Massacre Face

4 These routes involve significant steepness and often take place in well defined gullies rather than open bowls. Some (not all) of these routes will be steep enough to be described as a Grade I winter climb in the climbing guidebooks.

- **Adrenaline Scale:** Very Steep
- **Example Routes:** Forked Gully, Creag Dhubh Chute

5 These routes are very serious and will involve very steep, sustained, and sometimes exposed skiing. Only the most solid of skiers should try these routes as falls are likely to be punished severely. These routes will all be steep enough to be described as Grade I winter climbs in the climbing guidebooks, and some (not all) may have sections steep enough to be classed as Grade II. Some of these routes may require ropework and mountaineering skills to complete safely.

- **Adrenaline Scale:** Extremely Steep
- **Example Routes:** Boomerang, Summit Gully, Great Gully

X These routes are generally extremely tenuous and will hardly ever get skied. They become more like psychological challenges and tend to be undertaken during exceptional conditions by those with a need to test themselves. Often these routes will be classed as Grade II or even Grade III winter climbs.

- **Adrenaline Scale:** Good Luck
- **Example Routes:** None in this edition of the book

The variation brought by snow conditions can't be stressed strongly enough – for example a level 3 route on a sheet ice day will often be far more treacherous than a level 5 route on a spring snow day. In addition, remember that some of these routes will only have been done a small number of times (perhaps only once) and possibly in very unusual conditions – the grade is an indication only and you should always exercise your own judgement, expect the unexpected, and leave yourself plenty of safety margin.

Comparisons

Advice will sometimes be given to show other routes which are either similar in difficulty (or character), or harder. Along with the route's description this should help you better understand the difficulty rating for a particular route.

Combinations

Some routes are great when combined with other routes. Any combination suggestions are entirely optional.

Aspect / Slope Direction

The slope aspect is the direction it faces – so a gully with a Westerly aspect faces towards the West. When reading the avalanche forecast take careful note of the aspects (and heights) that they say will be most dangerous and choose routes accordingly. Each route description has an aspect icon that shows you roughly which direction a route faces in – this should make it easy to compare with the hazard 'compass rose' image displayed on the avalanche report. Make sure you read the exact wording of the report very carefully rather than just looking at the diagram.

Icons

Quality – the SkiMountain logo has been used to indicate a very subjective quality rating by the author. Three logos shows that this is a real favourite - a 'must do' route, while none shows a distinct lack of affection for the route!

Axe – You should have an axe and probably lightweight crampons with you to do this route. You may need them to get to the top of the route, or on the descent itself.

Skins – This icon indicates that you will find doing this route easier if you have skins and a touring setup. They are never essential, but may well make getting to or from the route easier.

Rope – This icon shows that you should seriously consider taking a rope and associated mountaineering equipment with you for this route. The description will tell you whether there are compulsory abseils involved (not many in this book) – sometimes you will be able to make the descent without needing the rope but carrying it just in case may be a sensible precaution. Of course one person's abseil is another's cliff hucking opportunity, so use your own judgement after reading the description to decide what equipment you need.

Note about Slope Angles

Many skiers put a lot of emphasis on the angle of a slope but this can change quite dramatically depending on snow build-up and also vary significantly through the length of the run. Even with an OS map and a magnifying glass, phone apps, inclinometers, or poles it is difficult to measure slope angles accurately and consistently so it can be quite a misleading way to describe a route. The difficulty of a route is always closely related to how steep it is, but also to its length, narrowness, how exposed it is, and how sustained it is. The combination of the grade, the description, and the comparisons with other routes should give you a better idea of how a particular run compares with others you have already done – ultimately that seems more useful than an angle.

Maps

All of the routes in this book are located in a corridor stretching roughly between Crianlarich and Ballachulish. There are several useful maps covering the area and which you choose may well depend on personal preference.

- 1:50k OS - Ben Nevis, Sheet 41 and Glen Orchy & Loch Etive, Sheet 50
- 1:40k Harvey's - Ben Nevis & Glen Coe
- 1:25k Harvey's - Glen Coe, Glen Etive & Black Mount
- 1:25k OS - Sheet 384 Glen Coe & Glen Etive, Sheet 377 Loch Etive & Glen Orchy

Each of the above has its merits – the classic red 1:50k OS maps are great but the split between sheets lies in the middle of the Black Mount. The Harvey's maps cover the best area for this book (apart from the Bridge of Orchy or Tyndrum hills) and these have the advantage of being lightweight and are made of waterproof material, although counting the 15metre contour lines (and 75m index contours) is sometimes too much for the author's mathematically limited brain.

Map, compass, GPS, altimeter

For anyone at all serious about doing much skiing in this area it is worth getting one or more of these maps, carrying a compass (and possibly a GPS and/or altimeter) and knowing how to use it all. There is also a free OS Map Reading leaflet which is often available in the outdoor shops beside the maps which will help keep you right about the tricky navigation required.

It is easy to get caught out in a whiteout or severe clag on top of these hills – Glencoe has a mixture of flat summit plateaus and narrow ridges on the summits, often with cliffs and cornices in close proximity. The key is to train yourself up and then try not to get lost in the first place! A watch altimeter is a particularly useful aid to navigation on skis, and can also provide a good morale booster when walking or skinning in (although don't look at it too often if you're going slowly). Remember with altimeters that all they can do is read the atmospheric pressure which is affected by changes in the weather as well as by height, so they need to be reset regularly whenever you're at a known height (e.g. at home, in the car park, at an obvious col, or on a summit).

Compass Interference

Be aware that many common objects can affect the reading of a compass – try waving your compass in front of your mobile phone, transceiver, or GPS and you will probably see the needle give the wrong reading. When you are using a compass make sure you hold it well away from any objects that will affect its reading. You should also be aware that prolonged proximity to such objects can semi-permanently knock your compass needle off-course, so store it somewhere sensible and be careful which bits of kit you put in the same pockets when on the hill.

Diagrams

GLENCOE CAR PARKS

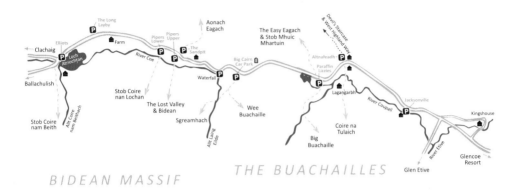

Most of the main sections of the book include at least one diagram showing you where the routes are. In most cases they have been oriented to face in the direction you are likely to approach the routes from. A few of the routes have GPS coordinates listed at the end of the book to help you find the right place and give you a bit more confidence about what you're dropping in to. The diagrams are used in preference to map extracts since they allow the key features to be highlighted, where necessary using a little artistic licence to accentuate certain features. A single constant scale is not used throughout, as stretching certain portions is often the only way to show useful details. Please note these are illustrations only and are not a substitute for maps, map reading, and common sense! The book is intended to be read and used alongside a map.

Weather and Snow Conditions

Although some of the hills in the Nevis mountain range just to the North of this book are slightly higher, the majority of the numerous mountains featured in this book all sit at around the 1000-1100metre mark. The snowline of some degree of reliability in this part of Scotland averages out at somewhere above 650metres, with reasonably frequent falls down to road levels, so in most seasons there is plenty of snowy mountainous terrain for the offpiste skier to choose from here.

Although seasons vary, dustings of snow tend to start appearing in late September. The first skiable dumps usually come during October, November or early December. Snow falling during October and November usually only lasts a few days before melting and there is rarely enough for a good base to develop. December and January (often into February) bring short days with frequently wild and windy weather in amongst further dumps of snow and / or rain, and every season these months bring intense speculation about whether it will be a good winter or not. If you time it just right or get lucky there can be some nice powder on offer during these early winter months.

Late February into March usually brings the most reliable ski conditions as by this time at least some sort of base has built up. April can be a great time for Scottish skiing, with longer and warmer days combined with spring snow. Most lifts usually close shortly after Easter because people stop turning up and buying tickets - but this time of year can bring fantastic touring conditions with the North and Eastern slopes often holding plenty of snow well through May and sometimes into June. The lifts have sometimes been kept running until the May Day holiday at the start of May, and a tradition of hiking up for mid-summer's day skiing on the 21st June (often in a kilt with a hip flask) is well and truly established.

Since it is warmed by the infamous Gulf Stream and North Atlantic Drift, this part of Scotland is very much warmer than other places sitting at 57° North. The height of our mountains and the corresponding prevailing temperatures here are such that there is a fine line between whether it snows or rains, and it is often a small variation that dictates whether it is a good season or not. It is unfortunately fairly common for it to be raining at car park level but snowing up high – the challenge being to stay dry until you are above the freezing level. Those in the know have been seen wearing

Time to get the skis out!

photo **Kenny Biggin**

photo **Blair Fyffe** | rider **Kenny Biggin**

an over-jacket and spare gloves on the Access Chair just for this purpose, while keeping your goggles tucked away out of the rain and sitting on your rucksack on the chair to keep your bum dry can also be good top tips.

The prevailing wind comes from the South West as low pressure systems spin out of the Atlantic and across the North of Scotland. A quick look at a map shows why this works so well in much of Glencoe, since the main mountain ridges are aligned almost perfectly at right angles to the prevailing wind (classic examples of North East aspects being loaded by South West winds). These long ridges create large deposition areas and encourage huge quantities of snow to collect in the North and Eastern corries.

Glencoe seems to be particularly prone to localised weather effects, and the wind can funnel down the glen even when none was forecast. Thankfully, the tows at Glencoe seem to be reasonably resilient to the wind. Because of the geography of the glen, the cloud can hang over the hills even when high pressure dominates and often in these circumstances it is well worth taking a look at the outlying hills, particularly Beinn a' Bheithir next to the coast as this will often have blue sky over it when others further down the glen stay obstinately shrouded.

Web Resources

There are a variety of good resources to check weather conditions, snow conditions, and what others have been up to. A few of the core ones are listed below, but there are many others so look around and find those that work well for you.

- Scottish Avalanche Information Service: www.sais.gov.uk
- Met Office Mountain Weather Forecast: www.metoffice.gov.uk
- Mountain Weather Information Service: www.mwis.org.uk
- Glencoe Mountain - www.glencoemountain.co.uk (keep an eye on their facebook page as well as their webcams)
- SkiMountain - www.SkiMountain.co.uk

Facebook pages and groups:

- /SkiMountain.co.uk
- British Backcountry group

Safety & Making Good Decisions

This book is part of a small series and each book contains varied but complimentary material about how to stay safe in the mountains. As well as reading this section you should also take a look at the safety information in the companion books. You should also consider going on an avalanche avoidance or mountain safety course and / or reading some of the many good books on the subject. Venturing into the mountains involves accepting a level of risk – that isn't to say you should become fatalistic about it, but rather you should do everything in your power to keep yourself safe while making sure you get out there as often as possible and enjoy yourself.

A Serious Place

There is some amazing skiing to be had here, but Glencoe has proved itself over the years to be a serious place. There are numerous high, steep, and rocky mountains, most of which are close to the road and within easy reach for the majority of the population. The prevailing weather, especially the temperature and the wind, dictates that snow conditions are constantly in flux, and the snowpack is continuously swinging from stable to unstable and back again. These factors have combined forces to catch many people out, and unfortunately the list of winter fatalities has grown quite long.

2013 was a horrible year for avalanches across Scotland, and Glencoe took its share of the pain which included several mountaineering deaths as well as the first offpiste skiing avalanche fatality

Scary! A weak layer lurking right at the bottom. The depth hoar snow crystals that have caused this form gradually during cold weather and a release could happen well after it last snowed. The two skiers that triggered this in 2010 were extremely lucky to get away with injuries and dented pride.

photo **Blair Fyffe**

A crown wall on the Spring Run – in the right conditions this is the gradient at which slopes can release

photo **Davy Gunn**

in recent memory (an event still very fresh and raw for many Glencoe locals). Despite the huge quantities of snow in 2014, somehow everyone managed to stay alive… however, there were enough incidents and close calls (including a number of people caught in slides on the Fly Paper) to know that it was probably luck rather than good sense that kept some people safe.

Even within the ski area there are a number of slopes capable of avalanching – the Fly Paper, Spring Run, Canyon, and The Wall have all avalanched. Ski Patrol assess these inbound slopes on a regular basis, and close them if required, but even here you should be tuned in to the potential.

Not Just Avalanches

While avalanches are without doubt an ever present danger, it's important not to forget about all the other aspects of staying safe in the mountains. Statistically, you are far more likely to get lost, get wet and cold, or simply fall over and injure yourself. Between the major hazards caused by ice, rocks, and crags there is more than enough to keep you on your toes. Make sure that you ski within your abilities, leaving yourself a respectful margin of safety. Take a fully charged mobile phone, and wear warm clothes and a helmet, as these simple precautions are your primary safety net should things start to go wrong. Depending what you are doing, make sure you have an appropriate selection of navigation and mountaineering equipment – especially when you are starting out in your offpiste career, it is far better to carry something (so long as it's light) and not need it, than to need it and not have it.

Margins of Safety

Without putting yourself off completely, try to have a little think about what might happen if something unexpected happens – for example you might catch an edge, tweak your knee, mess up a turn, or have a binding break on you halfway down a route. It is quite common to get into a route only to find you have misjudged snow conditions. These are things you should be able to handle and recover from, in a safe and controlled way, provided you haven't pushed things so close to the edge that there is no room left for error or bad luck.

Terrain Traps & Glencoe Chasms

The geology and geography of this area is such that there are an unusual number of major terrain trap features here. The three most noticeable features are similar in appearance and form massive gulches:

A massive terrain trap – skiing above such features should be reserved for irrefutably stable conditions

photo **Kenny Biggin**

- The Cam Ghleann Gorge under the Northwest flank of the ski hill
- The Lost Valley Gulch which lies just above the Lost Valley
- The Lairig Chasm below Coire Sgreamhach

The location of all of these are mentioned further within the book. Likewise, lochans in several corries, the gully at the exit of Coire na Tulaich, and the gulch below Beith Bowl, are other features capable of catching large volumes of debris and trapping unfortunate skiers. Of course there are many other smaller terrain traps, but those mentioned above are particularly worthy of caution.

Consequences - What's Below You?

Skiing in exposed positions, especially above cliffs or major terrain traps is a bold activity as even a small snow sluff (or fall) could have very serious consequences. Picking routes that offer great skiing, without exposing yourself to undue danger, is a good approach to foster. There are many open slopes and bowls here with fantastic skiing that are relatively inconsequential even if something does go wrong. Looking closely at the nature of the run out below your route is particularly important – long and gentle run out zones with gradual concave shapes are the things to look for. It is even possible to ski steep and hard routes without taking undue risks – the often heard sentiment amongst some of the more enlightened top skiers is:

"I like difficulty, but not danger... there is a difference."

photo **Blair Fyffe**

Mitigation

The bottom line when you are skiing offpiste is that you can't ever be one hundred percent sure what might happen, so routinely deploying a variety of mitigation steps and skiing defensively is a great practice to get into. Here are just a few of the most important:

- One at a time – as soon as you are in avalanche terrain, ski things one at a time (but never alone)
- Aim for safe zones – ridge tops, flat areas well out of the firing line, protected rock buttresses
- Treat all convex roll-overs with suspicion, and if you can leave them undisturbed, do so
- In gullies, stop well to the side and tucked in under buttresses – if you don't feel safe, you probably aren't
- Retain line-of-sight with your companions if it is safe to do so
- Don't linger, particularly in exposed positions like on scarp slopes or under cornices

When is it Stable?

Spring conditions are high on the list when it comes to thinking about stable snowpacks – here the snow tends to be well consolidated and yet offers great skiing. In the depths of winter, safe conditions are a little harder to find but waiting for some time since the last snow fall, during a prolonged mild spell with little wind present is a good bet.

© SkiMountain

Start off by aiming for the stable end of the spectrum, on the days when there can be little in the way of doubt, and then slowly expand your comfort zone as you gain more experience. This is a far less stressful route than approaching slope after loaded slope saying "hmm, is it potentially unstable today?" because the answer will almost always be yes.

The Avalanche Forecast

The SportScotland Avalanche Information Service (SAIS) provide avalanche forecasts throughout the winter months (usually from around mid December through to mid April) which can be accessed in a number of places including their website www.sais.gov.uk. The avalanche forecast is also posted in a number of other places including at the Glencoe ski area.

Reading the SAIS avalanche forecast the evening (or morning) before going skiing offpiste should become second nature. It tells you what the conditions were like when they were assessed, what the weather has done and will do, and it predicts what conditions you are likely to find. It can be very useful to look back at the preceding forecasts, weekly snowpack summaries, and the SAIS blog reports (which usually include photos) are particularly helpful for getting an idea of conditions before you arrive.

The SAIS Forecasts are based on thorough on the hill observations and a detailed, purpose produced weather forecast so they have a great track record of being correct and are the best starting point

The avalanche forecasters working hard in all conditions – the forecast is your starting point for good decision making

photo Kenny Biggin | rider Blair Fyffe

for your risk assessment. Once in a while the weather forecast will be slightly off (for instance stronger winds, more precipitation, warmer temperatures, or a different wind direction) and in those circumstances the avalanche forecast may also be slightly out - so they should be treated as a crucial part of your risk-assessment process but not as an excuse to stop thinking and taking responsibility for yourself. Most importantly, when you get to the top of a slope you must reassess the avalanche hazard and associated risks yourself using all the information at your disposal.

The compass-rose image in the information panel for each route is designed to make it easy to see which routes are likely to be avalanche prone on a particular day. As an example, you would be unwise to ski the Fly Paper on a day with the following avalanche forecast:

Bad Choice?

The precise wording of the avalanche reports are chosen very carefully, and by reading the reports regularly you can gain lots of extra information - take the time to understand in detail what the forecasters are describing. Make sure you read the avalanche report in full rather than just looking at the hazard diagram as the wording used should help you a lot with your decision making.

Decisions on the Hill

Before you leave your car, you should have done enough homework to know what the avalanche and weather forecasts say. So prior to getting to the snowline you should have a reasonably good idea of what to expect, which routes might be a good idea, and which areas are likely to be best avoided. Make sure that when you are reading the avalanche forecast you are mentally translating what it says onto the ground – if it says "hazardous on North Easterly aspects", take time to look at where that corresponds to on the mountain.

Look at your map and think about where the wind has been coming from and where snow is likely to have been deposited as a result. By looking at what temperatures are forecast you should get a good feel for how the snow might be changing at various levels – try to predict what the snow will be like once you're up there, and then see if you've got it right. Having a digital weather station in your living room at home and keeping an eye on what the temperature is doing in the evenings is a good way to have a better idea of what it's doing up the mountain. As a rough guide the temperature drops by a degree every 150metres (though the exact figure varies with humidity), so eight degrees at sea level results in freezing level near the tops at 1200metres. Remember that the snow will change during the day – windslab can build up over several hours, the sun can change an icy face to spring snow, and (in general) the longer you leave new snow to consolidate and stabilise the better.

Watch out for rapid thaws and rain – this avalanche scar on Stob a' Choire Odhair is from an end of season full depth release

photo **Joy Biggin** | rider **Paul Biggin**

Debris from a slab released 400metres higher up. Has there been enough time since the last storm cycle for the snow to consolidate? In Coire na Muic, Black Mount

photo **Kenny Biggin** | riders **Brian Morrison, Kevin Quinn, Ed Smith**

Once you're on the hill, start gathering information from everything you see and feel. In particular look for signs of windslab build-up, and telltale warning signs such as large cracks appearing in the snow as you tread on it. Look closely at the slopes you can see and note carefully any avalanche activity – recent debris is always a signal to raise your alertness levels.

Get into the habit of weighing up all the factors to do your own little risk assessment before skiing each route. There will almost always be a small level of risk, no matter what the conditions, but add too many danger factors to the equation and you may be pushing things to the tipping point where things could go very bad, very quickly.

The Tipping Point

Are you the trigger?

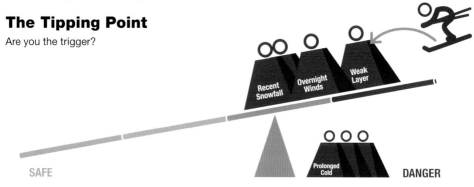

photo **Kenny Biggin**

Looks pretty but snow getting blown around is a sure sign that windslab will be forming (on Beinn an Dothaidh)

Recognising Windslab

By far the most common type of avalanche in Scotland is caused by windslab. Being able to recognise when and where windslab is present is a key skill to build into your repertoire. In fact, windslab being present is almost the norm in Scotland, but the problems arise when one layer of the snowpack slides on something under it. This happens when:

- The sliding layer is stuck together well enough to form a cohesive slab that can move as one
- There is a sliding surface underneath
- There isn't a strong enough bond between the slab and the sliding surface

With a little bit of experience you can start to look for the telltale signs of these three essential factors.

Is there a sliding surface?

The sliding surface can be the ground itself (for instance a grassy or scree covered slope); a layer of ice; a layer of ball-bearing like hailstones or 'graupel'; a layer of weak snow crystals (depth hoar or buried surface hoar); or even a differing layer of snow.

Is there a slab?

It is tricky to tell whether you are skiing on windslab or not as it doesn't necessarily 'feel' like windslab. Although there is a whole spectrum of variations, there are actually two main types of slab – 'hard' and 'soft' – and they feel completely different to ski on. Soft windslab is usually a bit more obvious as it frequently breaks into blocks as you weight it – you can also scrape your hand through it relatively easily to see what it is sitting on. Hard windslab catches people out and to the unwary can feel completely stable as it feels very solid under you – however there could be a large layer of snow tightly packed together sitting on top of a weak layer... this scenario can result in large avalanches with devastating results.

photo **Kenny Biggin** | rider **Scott Muir**

Evidence of recent avalanche activity is a major warning sign

photo **Kenny Biggin** | rider **Katie Fleming**

At the end of the season, beware of cornice, ice, and rock debris falling from above as the thaw sets in

The Tricky Bit

It has been said that experience is something that you gain on the days when you survive to tell the tale. The more experience you gain, the more you realise how fragile the line can be between a great day and a disastrous one. Often experienced mountaineers and skiers will say that to a large extent they rely on a sixth sense, or gut feeling, to help them make go or no-go decisions. These gut feelings aren't actually as mystical as they sound – they are the accumulation of hundreds of days in the mountains, in tandem with lots of reading, training, thinking, and of course a few close calls. Building up your brain's own expert system should be your aim, and often shortcuts to help you get there safely include skiing with more experienced people, asking lots of questions, but most importantly being inquisitive and getting out there as often as possible and paying attention to the snow.

The tricky bit, however, isn't building up knowledge and experience… it is knowing when not to ignore it. Recognising danger is hard, but turning back is harder. There have been many cases of relatively experienced people who have skied into danger, probably knowing full well that they are flying close to the wind. The temptation of pristine snow is frequently too hard to ignore. The trouble is that often you will get away with ignoring your instincts, and you never know how close to disaster you actually were. Make a point of listening to your gut feelings and turning back – saying no once in a while when things don't feel right is a good habit to get into, and one which might help you dodge a bullet one of these days.

Never stop building up your awareness of what you're skiing on

photo **Kenny Biggin** | rider **Neil Muir**

Myths Debunked

Let's take a look at some frequently heard discussion topics and some responses.

1. "Wearing a helmet / transceiver / airbag makes you more likely to do something dangerous"
This could be seen as very much like driving on the road – in general, skiing offpiste is a relatively safe activity and avalanche incidents are comparatively rare (similar to the relationship driving on roads has with car crashes). You don't drive off in your car thinking: "I'd better not put my seatbelt on in case it encourages me to do something dangerous".

So there shouldn't be any reason why putting your transceiver or helmet on should encourage you to act recklessly – they should just be an integral part of your skiing kit, as is the case with wearing your seatbelt when driving. Problems arise when people only wear this equipment some of the time – this is a bad habit that encourages a mentality of mitigating danger by wearing extra equipment. The equipment (whether it's a seatbelt or a helmet or transceiver) should be worn as standard attire as a precaution, while the danger is mitigated through good decision making and careful driving.

Having said that, if you keep finding yourself at the top of cornices thinking:

"Screw it… it'll probably slide but I'll be fine, I've got my tranny on."

…then it might be time to take a long hard look at your decision making skills. To continue the analogy, you don't embark on a dangerous overtake on a blind corner thinking "it'll be fine, I've got my seatbelt on", so don't apply this mentality to skiing.

2. "In many avalanche fatalities in Scotland, trauma is the killer and wearing a transceiver wouldn't have made any difference"
This is absolutely true and a good reason to stay away from rocks, cliffs, and wear a helmet plus lots of clothes, but not a reason to get into bad habits. Even without looking abroad, there are enough incidents in Scotland where a transceiver 'might' have helped to save avalanche victims. Transceivers are easy to wear, long lasting, and not really that expensive relative to the rest of your ski expenditure, so there isn't a good reason not to wear one. If you're still not convinced, remember that you aren't solely wearing your transceiver to save yourself, but also to be able to search for your buddies if it all goes wrong. If you are one day in the horrible situation of standing at the top of a slope looking down at a bunch of avi debris with your mate somewhere underneath it, wouldn't you like to be able to get your transceiver out and at least have a chance of getting them out.

For the long term psychological benefit of the survivors and searchers, wearing transceivers and being able to do your best for the people you're with, is yet another powerful argument for making this kit standard issue.

Standard Kit

If you intend to ski offpiste you should wear a helmet and a turned on transceiver, and carry a small light rucksack with a shovel and probe in it. All too often people skiing around the ski hill can be asked "fancy coming to ski x,y,z with us - have you got your avi kit with you?" only to hear the reply "Nah, didn't know whether I'd go offpiste today so didn't bother". This is a good way to get caught out as the temptation of hearing your buddies tell you how great it is will usually be too strong to resist. Get into the habit of taking your kit with you just in case – you can always leave your rucksack somewhere while you do a few laps on the pistes.

Once you own this kit, make a habit of using it every time you go skiing - irrespective of what the conditions are or what you think your plan is. Put your transceiver on when you put your salopettes on and turn it on at the same time (i.e. at breakfast). Do not turn it off until you are back home or in the pub. Replace the batteries regularly – as a matter of course at the start of each season and then keep an eye on the battery meter. Why not keep the battery percentage up above 90% - batteries are cheap. As important as owning and wearing this kit is knowing how to use it quickly and efficiently – take a course and make a point of practising every season (if only to make sure your companions will be able to find you quickly!)

Transceiver Check

Part of your daily offpiste skiing routine should become a transceiver check – an efficient way to do this is in two stages:

- Stage 1: Before you leave the carpark, do a transceiver check with your buddies (apart from anything else, this makes sure no-one has forgotten to put theirs on before you get further up the hill). Start off by standing some distance away from your group with your beacon on transmit while everyone else walks towards you on search hopefully demonstrating they can find you). Everyone should now turn their beacons to transmit.
- Stage 2: Whoever is first off the Main Basin T-bar (or first to the snowline if skinning up) heads off away from the group and turns their transceiver to receive, then the rest of the group ski slowly past you at intervals so that you can check they are transmitting and that your beacon can pick them up. Make sure you finish the process by turning your own beacon back to transmit.

This simple two stage process keeps hassle to a minimum while ensuring everyone is wearing a turned on fully functioning transceiver and has at least a basic understanding of how to use it.

Transceiver Park

There is a transceiver training park up the lifts at Glencoe and this is a great thing to do if you find yourself on your own or with some spare time, perhaps when conditions elsewhere are less than perfect.

Finding your Buddies

If (despite all the great decisions you've made) the worst happens and you get avalanched, the most likely thing to save you (assuming you've worn your helmet, warm clothes, transceiver, zorbing suit etc.) is speedy and efficient actions by your friends. So make sure you ski with folk who carry transceiver, shovel, and probe and practise regularly with them so you know you are skiing with people who you can count on.

The most likely way for a person to survive burial is for their companions to dig them out fast. In the cold light of day in your back garden or on a course, searching seems easy and the risks seem fairly abstract… however, anyone who has had a close call will tell you that it is extremely scary and staying calm, rational, and efficient is difficult at best. Do not waste valuable time going back to tell ski patrol or phoning for help at this point unless it can be done with a very quick shout or in parallel by other people. Your buddy's best chance is YOU.

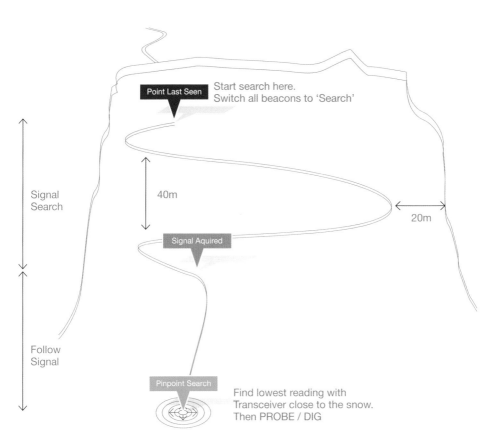

Point Last Seen

Start search here.
Switch all beacons to 'Search'

Signal
Search

40m

20m

Signal Aquired

Follow
Signal

Pinpoint Search

Find lowest reading with
Transceiver close to the snow.
Then PROBE / DIG

As the avalanche happens, try to keep your eyes on the victim for as long as possible, then as soon as the slope stops moving check it is safe to move yourself and go straight to the spot they were last seen. Tell the other skiers you're with to turn their transceivers to Search as well (most have an 'autorevert' function to switch them back to transmit after a while in case of a secondary avalanche) and tell them to hang back but get their probes and shovels ready for use.

From the spot the victim was last seen get your transceiver out, switch to Search mode and begin a search. The exact technique varies depending which transceiver you have, and recommendations evolve over time. However, the basic process goes as follows.

Find Signal: Zig zag systematically down the avi path until you pick up an initial signal. Make sure you cover the entire slide path never leaving gaps of more than 15-20metres.

Follow Signal In: As soon as you pick up the signal, follow the signal in rapidly until you are within a few metres. Be quick but be careful not to go so fast that you muck this part up – it's all too easy on a steep slope to suddenly realise you've shot 20metres too low and wading back up will take ages.

Pinpoint: Take your skis off and hold your transceiver low right next to the snow in a cross shape to do a pinpoint search and mark the lowest reading with a pole. Accuracy here will save you time later.

Probe: Having found the lowest reading, whip your probe out and methodically probe around your marker in a gradually widening circular pattern until you find the body. Push your probe in at right angles to the slope rather than vertically. Do not be tempted to skip the probing stage as it has been shown to dramatically reduce the time digging, even in a shallow burial. Leave your probe in place on the body and get your shovel out.

Dig: It has been shown that there is a real art to how to dig a victim out most efficiently, but in essence the best way is to dig in into the slope to them rather than down. If there are multiple helpers position them behind you to help clear the snow out of the way as you dig.

Clear Airway & Revive: As soon as you find the body, try to clear the face and airway as fast as possible. If required give them some rescue breaths and begin CPR to keep their blood pumping – make sure help is on its way pronto!

There are a variety of other techniques to learn and practise when it comes to searching for buried victims – for instance multiple burials, or if there are multiple searchers. These are best learnt on a course, but make sure you put most of your effort into learning how to avoid getting into trouble, rather than how to get out of it.

Getting Help

You should always try to be self sufficient and resolve incidents yourself if you can, but also recognise when you need help. If the worst should happen, stabilise the situation as much as you can and then contact any of the following (either yourself or via someone else) and give them as much information as possible.

Ski Patrol – can be contacted via radio by asking the lifty at the bottom of all tows. The patrol hut at the bottom of the Main Basin T-bar is also permanently manned. Running into the café shouting will usually illicit a response as well. Even if you are outside the ski area boundary, if you have used the lifts to get up there contacting ski patrol is a good place to start – they will have this book and will have knowledge about where you say you are and if necessary will be able to coordinate contacting external help from the police or mountain rescue if required. Although they will always do their best for you, don't expect Ski Patrol to be able to come to your aid if you are offpiste – their primary responsibility is looking after the people on the front of the mountain, and may not have enough staff to help out elsewhere. Be aware that the weekend patrollers at Glencoe are volunteers, so be nice!

Glencoe Mountain Resort – phone 01855 851 226 which will take you through to the ticket office. They have radio contact with ski patrol. Put this number in your phone now!

Police / Mountain Rescue Team – in an emergency contact the police directly by dialling 999. Tell them where you are, what's happened, and that you are likely to need the Mountain Rescue Team. If you are near the lifts make sure you tell them you're at the Glencoe ski hill, and if you can give them a grid reference, route name from this book, or GPS location even better. Even if it looks like you haven't got a mobile signal, you can sometimes still get through to 999. If you have registered your mobile in advance and find yourself unable to call, you can also send a text message to 999 – register your phone now simply by texting 'register' to 999 (more info at www.emergencysms.org.uk).

Glencoe Mountain Rescue Team (GMRT) is entirely operated by volunteers and the team survives on donations and good will. They deal with around eighty call-outs a year already, so use them as a last resort and support them any way you can – you can start by taking a look at their website www.glencoemountainrescue.org.uk which has a link allowing you to make donations. On the more Northerly hills, Lochaber Mountain Rescue Team may well attend. The neighbouring teams of Oban, Arrochar, and Killin may also become involved in rescues in the book's area, particularly on the Bridge of Orchy and Tyndrum hills.

Glencoe Mountain Resort – Meall a' Bhuiridh

Over sixty years before this book was written, intrepid skiers from across Scotland were gradually working out where the best places to ski were. No doubt many of the mountains described in this book were initially explored by these early offpiste freeriders, and we owe the sport that we know now to what the visionaries amongst them did next. Chief amongst them was Philip Rankin who had the foresight to see that what Scottish skiers badly needed was a snow sure and easily accessible mountain with a fixed lift system on it. He looked long and hard for the perfect location and eventually settled on the slopes of Meall a' Bhuiridh in Glencoe. The rest is history – Philip led the charge to build the first fixed lifts in Scotland here and in 1956 the Glencoe ski area opened to the public and hasn't looked back since.

Of course there have been a couple of hiccups along the way, not helped by the string of bad snow years around the turn of the century, but five years ago the current owner Andy Meldrum took the reigns firmly by the hand and the future of Glencoe Mountain Resort seems in good shape. There are many exciting development plans afoot and it is likely that the piste and lift map shown in this book may well need to be updated before too long. Investment is being made upgrading the infrastructure including the hill's electrics and huts. A new dry slope, an additional beginners lift, and the possibility of a new chair, will all help modernise the lift system and improve capacity. Meanwhile plans to build an enormous Zipline (running from close to the top of the Access Chair) which will operate year round are taking shape giving real hope that the future of the resort will be secure for a long time to come.

This is the oldest ski resort in Scotland, and there is a certain unpretentious charm to the place that goes hand in hand with the strong feeling of camaraderie that is the epitome of the Glencoe skiing community's mentality. They all know there are bigger mountains and better lift systems abroad, with more consistent snow and more sunny days, but land yourself a good day skiing at Glencoe and you will realise why many skiers are so fiercely proud of their local resort. As has been said elsewhere, Glencoe lays a strong claim to the title of "The Best Wee Ski Area in the World".

There is a little more info on the history of skiing in Glencoe at the back of the book.

Front-side

Although this is an offpiste guidebook, it is worthwhile taking a whistle-stop tour of the lift and piste system at Glencoe, since the offpiste is almost always best done in conjunction with some runs on the front of the mountain. When you turn off the main A82 road onto the access road that leads up to the car park, it is worth stopping in one of the passing places for a minute and taking a look at the mountain. The access road takes you up to the car park at around 370metres high. At the far end of the car park there is the ticket office, ski hire, toilets, and Café Ossian which provides an excellent coffee at the start of the day and a beer at the end.

Behind Café Ossian, the Access Chair rises up above 650metres which is often around the right level

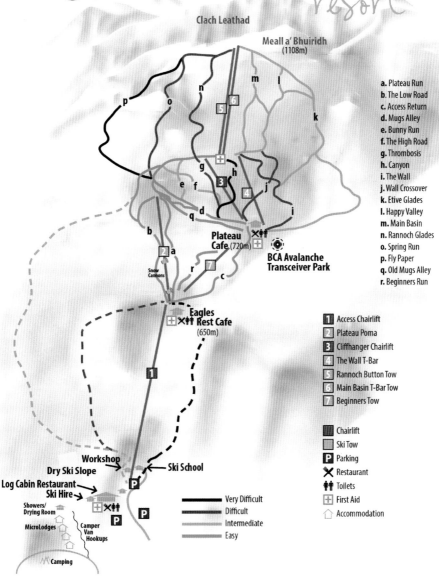

glencoe mountain
resort

Clach Leathad

Meall a' Bhuiridh
(1108m)

m l

n

p

o

5 6

k

g

e f 3 h

4 j

q d

b

i

2 a

Snow
Cannons

r 7

c

**Plateau
Cafe** (720m)

**BCA Avalanche
Transceiver Park**

**Eagles
Rest Cafe**
(650m)

1

Workshop
Dry Ski Slope

Ski School

Log Cabin Restaurant
Ski Hire

P

Showers/
Drying Room

P

P

MicroLodges

**Camper
Van
Hookups**

Camping

a. Plateau Run
b. The Low Road
c. Access Return
d. Mugs Alley
e. Bunny Run
f. The High Road
g. Thrombosis
h. Canyon
i. The Wall
j. Wall Crossover
k. Etive Glades
l. Happy Valley
m. Main Basin
n. Rannoch Glades
o. Spring Run
p. Fly Paper
q. Old Mugs Alley
r. Beginners Run

1 Access Chairlift
2 Plateau Poma
3 Cliffhanger Chairlift
4 The Wall T-Bar
5 Rannoch Button Tow
6 Main Basin T-Bar Tow
7 Beginners Tow

Chairlift
Ski Tow
P Parking
Restaurant
Toilets
First Aid
Accommodation

Very Difficult
Difficult
Intermediate
Easy

skimountain

to get to the snow line. Beside the top of the Access Chair there is a small café and toilet block just below the bottom of the Plateau Poma. This button tow runs gently across the long and reasonably flat area that leads up to where the main skiing starts. On the odd occasion when there isn't enough snow for the poma to run, you can have to walk across a track for ten minutes from here to get across the plateau.

At the top end of the plateau, there is a café with toilets, the Glencoe Ski Club hut, and the base of the single man Cliffhanger Chairlift. Close by is the bottom of the Wall T-bar. These two lifts take you up to the mid-height level on the mountain where the ski patrol and the Scottish Ski Club huts are located. There is some nice skiing in this central part of the mountain including Mugs Alley, Thrombosis, The Canyon (which forms a fantastic natural half-pipe), The Bum (or Bomb) Hole under the bottom of the Cliffy where many skiers have taken their first jumps (and their best falls), and The Wall to the right of the t-bar as you look up it.

The top part of the mountain is served by two lifts that run side by side – the Rannoch Button and the Main Basin T-bar. From the offpiste perspective these tows are crucial, although there are also some excellent piste runs here as well. As you're looking up at the mountain, the Fly Paper is the steep line on the left hand side of the hill, while the Spring Run and Rannoch Glades are the two main lines of snow in between here and the top lifts. There can also be nice skiing right beside the Rannoch Button and this run is known as the Rock Garden, for obvious reasons. To looker's right of the top lifts there is the Main Basin which has the iconic Haggis Trap feature at the bottom of it. The Haggis Trap is a deep chasm which in most seasons is a very obvious feature, and good fun to ski through, but in big snow years such as 1994 and 2014 it has been known to completely fill in and be buried.

Beside the Main Basin there is also a run called Happy Valley and beyond that the Etive Glades piste runs all the way down the looker's right hand ridge line to the bottom of the Wall T-bar. One nice run favoured by in-the-know locals links Happy Valley with The Wall via 'The Waterfall'. There are many pleasing variations of the main routes, and people will often say they particularly enjoy Glencoe skiing because of the interesting terrain.

Glencoe Lift Etiquette

Over the last sixty years since the lifts opened, Scottish skiers have developed a fantastic litany of traditions and procedures that (most of the time) help keep the skiers happy and the lift system running smoothly. Even on busy days it is possible, with a pinch of patience, to get up the hill fairly quickly if you know the score. If aliens landed on planet Earth at the bottom of the Wall T-bar with the aim of studying our culture, they might at first be slightly bemused at what they saw. Hopefully the summary below will help keep the little green men (new to our planet) amongst you right.

The exceptional snow in 2014 completely buried the Patrol hut

photo **Blair Fyffe**

AT TOP
PLEASE
HOLD T-BAR
UNTIL IT
RETRACTS

The famous Haggis Trap at the bottom of the Main Basin

photo **Doug Bryce** | rider **Doug Paton**

skimountain

- **"Single"**

  T-bars are designed to carry two people up the hill at once, so leaving one half of a bar empty is a waste of uplift capacity. If you are about to get on a t-bar and realise that you have no-one to share it with, shout "Single" loudly. Of course doing this in most social situations would be a pretty good way of getting laughed at, but in Scottish lift queues it is perfectly acceptable and some eagle eared local will race out of the queue and be down next to you passing the time of day in seconds. For the snowboarders amongst you look out for the variations to the traditional shout: "Goofy Single" and "Regular Single". As in life, the sooner you anticipate being a single and pair up with someone, the better.

- **"New Queue"**

  Instead of having queues that stretch halfway up the already fairly short runs, it is customary to regularly start New Queues. There is no exact science to this but typically if you come down a run and think "I'm not stopping there" when you see the top of the queue, it may be time to ski to the bottom and shout loudly "New Queue". Keep things as neat as you can and it sometimes helps keep things in order to place a back-marker at the end of the old queue to make sure anyone trying to join there is told to go and join the new queue instead. It is not unknown for there to be multiple short queues, one behind the other. As soon as the old queue depletes enough having gone up the lift, the new queue slides forward and becomes the establishment (it's another metaphor for life!)

- **"I've got the bar"**

  This one is used on any t-bar, but in particular it is important on tows which have a bull wheel close to where you get off the tow. In these cases the last person off the tow should keep hold of the bar until its pulley goes around the wheel, and then feed the rope back in before letting go, so that it doesn't either get tangled and cause the tow to stop, or clobber someone on the head.

- **"Stay on the Track"**

  Old ski lifts are sensitive souls and it is all too easy to derail the cable off the wheels on the pylons. Don't weave wildly out to the sides as you're going up the tow otherwise a weary patroller, tired of fixing de-rails, may remind you to "Stay on the track".

- **"Empty"**

  Someone misses a t-bar or poma and shouts "Empty" so that someone poaching can be quick and grab it, maximising efficiency. You should be wary of doing this though, as it is a good way of stressing both the tows and patrollers.

photo **Doug Bryce**

Glencoe Ski Club hut in the foreground – the Canyon is the obvious deep gully with the Patrol Hut and Main Basin above and the Cliffy Chair to the left

Alan Baillie getting some laps in

photo **Kenny Biggin** | rider **Alan Baillie**

New Queue!

photo **Kenny Biggin** | rider **Gregor Muir**

Why should the paralympians in Socchi have all the fun? Gregor trying out the alternatives while a leg operation heals

Welcome
to Scotland's
first ski resort.

Got a ticket to ride?

Fàilte dhan chiad
Ionad-sgithidh
an Alba.

Tiogaid agad ri rùid?

Glencoe
MOUNTAIN RESORT

The iconic Cliffy Chairlift with The Wall behind

photo **Stephen Speirs**

CLIFFHANGER
CHAIRLIFT

Pristine freshies on The Wall

The Cliffy with Plateau Café below - a chairlift designed over 50 years ago, still going strong!

Blue sky and snow to the car park - The Access Chair with the CD Shoulder on the right

The Access

The Glencoe Mountain Resort car park lies at around 370metres, so although it is far from the norm it is relatively common to have snow lying all the way down. In many ways, this was part of what made Meall a' Bhuiridh an attractive location for a ski resort, since the main road was high enough to provide good access to the snow line without being so high as to suffer enforced snow closures too often. The nature of the terrain above the car park has the added advantage of being at a great angle for skiing and predominantly consisting of grass and heather, without too many rocks, allowing skiers to enjoy these slopes without the need for too much of a base.

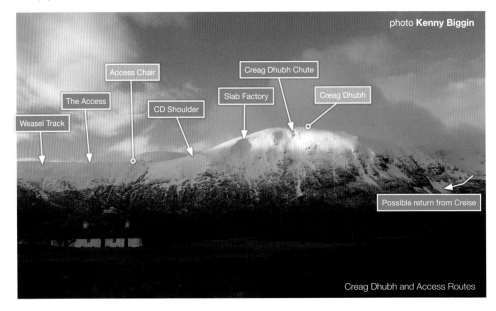

Access Chair

Creag Dhubh Chute

The Access

Slab Factory

Creag Dhubh

CD Shoulder

Weasel Track

Possible return from Creise

Creag Dhubh and Access Routes

1. The Access

The classic access route is a fantastic ski, suitable for a wide range of abilities, and this route is of course a great way to end a day's skiing on the lifts. The route starts by going out to skier's right at the top of the access chairlift and follows the line of a snowfence that travels the majority of the way down the hill to just above the car park. The easiest skiing lies to the skier's right of the snowfence although a wide variety of different lines are possible. If there isn't quite enough snow you may well have to walk the bottom third of the route, so be prepared to get your boots a little muddy!

2. Access Chair

harder than: The Access

An excellent variation of the classic access route is to ski a line almost directly underneath the access chairlift. The ground is slightly steeper here with a variety of small gully lines and interesting dips and rolls. Be careful not to stray too close to the bank of the burn as it contains some big cliffs and waterfalls which you would not want to fall over. You can drop into this line from skier's left of the bottom of the Plateau Tow, passing the buildings to your right and cruising over the flat headwaters of the burn aiming roughly towards the chairlift, aiming to meet it as the ground begins to steepen. If the snow starts to run out lower down, the best option is usually to break out towards the snowfence to your right where a little more snow may prolong your run and preserve your bases.

3. Weasel Track

similar to:	The Access
combine with:	East Ridge

A great easy angled adventure to end the day's skiing with is to head way out to skier's right of the classic access route. The run is named after the old ex-army tracked vehicles – 'Weasels' – which were used to transport equipment for the first ski tows up the mountain via this route. You can head out this way from the top of the Access Chair, but an even nicer option is to start the journey to skier's right of the top of the Plateau Tow, or perhaps up higher on The East Ridge. Fewer people venture out this way yet the skiing can be superb in good snow. The choice of line is entirely up to you – further right (East) tends to be gentler and if you get the urge you could keep going until you hit the West Highland Way before doing a flat traverse back towards the access road. The only thing to be aware of is that you should be aiming in a roughly North Westerly direction rather than heading so far right that you start going East which would start to take you down towards Ba Cottage instead.

photo **Stephen Speirs**

Tracks galore on the Access

Creag Dhubh

This iconic little foothill must be one of the best known and loved sights in Scottish skiing. As you drive up the well worn access road on a snowy day, Creag Dhubh beckons the skier with pristine snowy flanks, a tempting gully, and a taste of the day to come. Creag Dhubh is the prominent bump that lies up and to looker's right of the Access Chair, and at 748metres high its upper slopes are plenty high enough to hold onto skiable snow for much of a good season.

4. Creag Dhubh Chute

harder than:	Slab Factory
combine with:	Etive Glades

This is a classic run that should be on every aspiring offpiste skier's hit list. It is incredibly obvious from the access road and car park but even then doesn't get skied as often as you might expect. It is of course plenty steep and high enough for avalanches, and although it never gets all that narrow, it undoubtedly has enough of an angle to have given many people pause for thought... but after all, that's part of the fun! Like most routes in this book it is not a pleasant place if either icy or unstable.

On top of Creag Dhubh

photo **Kenny Biggin** | rider **Brian Morrison**

The entrance to the chute is actually slightly tricky to find – the best way of getting to it is to come down the Etive Glades from the top of The Wall or from the summit. As the Etive Glades starts to flatten out, stay out on the ridge well to skier's left of the bottom of the Wall T-bar. Cruise over the shallow col in the ridge and head for the summit of Creag Dhubh. There are a number of little cairns on the summit plateau so they don't really help you much – the top of the chute lies further left than you probably imagine, and starts slightly below the summit as the ground starts to drop away. Do a couple of traverses left and right if you're not sure – the entrance is obvious once you find it.

There is usually a bit of a convex rollover to get into the main gully, after which some good jump turns will spit you out onto the open, but still fairly steep, slopes. If there is enough snow you can continue straight down below the bottom of the chute until you either run out of snow or can traverse back to the car park. If the snow runs out fairly early it is often best to cut out right after exiting the gully and traverse back towards the burn under the Access Chair.

5. Slab Factory

harder than:	CD Shoulder
combine with:	Etive Glades

Lying to skier's right of the Creag Dhubh Chute is another part of these slopes that helped earn the hill the name 'White Corries'. Like the Chute, snow tends to hang around on at least the upper parts of this North Easterly slope fairly well. Rolling off the summit slopes of Creag Dhubh, there is a steep slope and mini-bowl here which can often form a cornice and windslab. There is more good skiing here on the right day and if the mist is down but the snow is low this can be a nice route to add to your Access laps. If you don't fancy going higher up the mountain to come into this from Etive Glades, it is reasonably easy to get to from the top of the Access Chair with a short hike or skin. If you are finding the slope too steep for your liking, keep heading back over to skier's right to reach the easier slopes on the CD Shoulder.

The Creag Dhubh Chute - the ski area car park below

The name of this route comes from the fact that even though it's fairly low, windslab releases are reasonably frequent here and skiers and boarders have been caught in slides both here and in the Creag Dhubh Chute.

6. CD Shoulder

harder than: Access Chair

As you travel up the Access Chair on a nice snowy day after sleeping in, you will regularly see someone poaching what should have been your tracks over to looker's right of the burn. The slope angle is a bit steeper here than on the access routes to the East of the chairlift, and when the snow is low enough this route is a great introduction to slightly steeper offpiste skiing with a bit of heather hopping thrown in. The best way of dropping in to this run is to ski down the Plateau run and keep heading down the fall line to skier's left. You can go further to the left with a bit of a traverse to get onto the shoulder a bit higher up or drop straight down keeping the burn to your right.

Looking up to the Slab Factory and the exit of the Creag Dhubh Chute

photo Kenny Biggin

The Fly Paper & Beyond

As you glide across the Plateau on the poma, the slope directly above is the Spring Run, while the steeper slope to looker's left is the Fly Paper. There are a number of fantastic runs on this Easterly part of Meall a' Bhuiridh, some easy... others less so. In recent years this area has been the location of the Coe Cup freeride competition, with the start gate at the top of the face and the judges gazing up from the bottom.

photo **Kenny Biggin**

Top Tows
Rannoch Glades
Spring Run
Fly Paper
Radio / Baillies
The East Ridge
Ba Burn
Mugs Alley
Plateau Poma

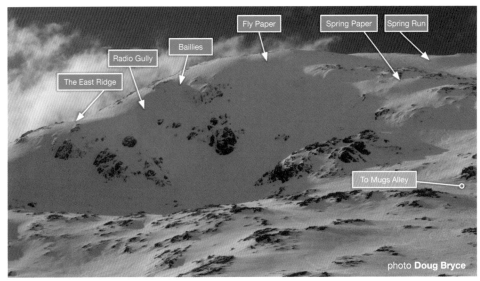

Fly Paper
Spring Paper
Spring Run
Baillies
Radio Gully
The East Ridge
To Mugs Alley

photo **Doug Bryce**

© SkiMountain

7. Fly Paper

harder than: Spring Run

Undoubtedly one of the best known Scottish ski run names, and often one that lays claim to the title of steepest Scottish piste, the Fly Paper is a great asset to the Glencoe ski hill and a brilliant piece of route naming. Perhaps more so than any other, the Fly Paper has become a true part of Scottish skiing folklore. Skiing it often becomes a right of passage for many as their first foray onto 'steep' slopes and black runs. Indeed the Fly Paper is actually quite deserving of respect as it is a fierce undertaking when icy and in certain snow conditions can be quite prone to avalanche.

The Fly Paper lies to skier's right of the front of the Glencoe ski hill, with the Spring Run providing a slightly easier run to try out prior to committing to this. Access the Fly Paper by taking one of the top tows (Rannoch Button or Main Basin T-bar) and get off to your left at the top. A quick few side steps or short pole will help get you onto the boulder lined path that Charlie Kennedy built. This path often holds enough snow to let you traverse through the rock strewn slope until you come out at the top of the Spring Run. After skiing a few turns, instead of continuing down the Spring Run, the Fly Paper takes you slightly further to skier's right where the ground starts to drop away onto an obviously

Freshies on the Fly

photo **Doug Bryce** | rider **Doug Paton**

⚠ skimountain

Sweet turns and soft landings

photo **Stephen Speirs** | rider **Malachai Hough**

steeper slope. Carry on down the slope as best you can until the gradient mellows at which point you can traverse back to the left to meet the edge of Mugs Alley.

Author's Note: During the 2014 season when this book was written, the author counted at least three separate incidents of skiers or boarders being caught in significant windslab releases here – thankfully all were OK but caution is advised, particularly after fresh snow or overnight South Westerly winds. There have been a number of close calls here over the years, including one skier who was dug out alive after being completely buried apart from a hand sticking out, and another who was buried up to his neck and sustained back injuries, so be careful. When you are in the backcountry away from the lifts (and out of sight of people who will follow your example) you are free to make your own decisions, but this is an in-bounds run within easy viewing of the public and as such you should try hard to respect whether Ski Patrol have deemed it safe or not. At least go and have a chat to ski patrol first as they may well have a reason that you don't know about for closing things.

Avalanche advice outside the Ski Patrol hut

Pushing hard in the Coe Cup

photo Stephen Speirs | rider Alistair Waley

8. Baillies Gully

2

| harder than: | Fly Paper |
| combine with: | Radio Gully |

Named after long time ski patroller Alan Baillie (though one couldn't possibly comment on the story behind it). To skier's right of the Fly Paper, there is a rocky buttress that lies in the middle of the bowl. To the right of the buttress, this great little route drops down between the rocks into the steep bowl and joins up with Radio Gully. As with the Fly Paper, the route shouldn't be taken lightly but in the right conditions this run provides superb lift served offpiste skiing.

9. Radio Gully

similar to:	Fly Paper
combine with:	Baillies

Really just another variation to the Fly Paper, this open gully at the far edge of the ski hill provides an exciting route into the steep bowl from skier's right. The best way to get into it is to ski the top section of the East Ridge and then drop to your left through some rocks where you will find the edge of the steeper section. The name comes from the time a ski patroller, who shall remain nameless, lost his radio here and had a long fruitless time searching for it in the hope of avoiding the inevitable stick from his comrades. Other patrollers will take great pleasure in telling you this is far from the only location that radios have been lost in! There is a fair amount of debate as to exactly where the distinction between Radio Gully and Baillies lies, and perhaps the best person to put the debate to rest is to ask the man himself.

Ski Patroller's privileges - fresh tracks in Radio Gully

photo **Keith Hill** | rider **Christine Hill**

© SkiMountain

10. The East Ridge

harder than: Etive Glades

combine with: Ba Cottage, Weasel Track

Carving through the clouds on the East Ridge

photo **Doug Bryce** | rider **Grigor Browning**

The East Ridge marks the far left hand edge of the 'front' of the Glencoe ski hill as you look up, and as it snakes its way down the skyline if offers a really classy offpiste run in a great setting. Amongst locals, this is a real favourite as it has all the right ingredients without ever being too serious. The route is easily accessed by continuing past the top of the Spring Run and Fly Paper and then simply carrying on down the nicely angled slopes on the ridge line with the steep ground of Baillies and Radio Gully safely on your left. You can continue down for around 200metres of great descent before needing to think about traversing back round to skier's left to travel underneath the bottom of the steep Fly Paper slopes to get back to the lifts. It is common to cut left fairly early to drop into the remainder of the steep bowl underneath Radio Gully. If the snow is low enough and you fancy the adventure, why not make it a really long run and continue all the way down to Ba Cottage?

Boarding heaven on the East Ridge

photo **Stephen Speirs** | rider **Ross Murray**

11. Ba Cottage

similar to:	The Access
combine with:	East Ridge, Baillies, Monument

Hidden from sight from the main pistes, there is an adventurous yet fairly easy offpiste run dropping invitingly away to the South East of Coire Pollach where the main skiing takes place. The route takes you low down a good distance away from the lifts or car park so good low snow cover and ideally skins and touring setup are needed in order for this to be a good option. Although it is possible to access the top of this route from the Cliffhanger Chair, or even from the top of the Plateau Tow, a far better and longer option is to combine it with a run down the East Ridge, Baillies, or even one of the South Face routes such as Doon Ra Ba or Monument. The run follows the line of a broad gully which holds a burn that flows down to the ruined Ba Cottage. The route is wide open and choice of line is not important.

Once down at the cottage you have several options to extricate yourself. One route is to follow the line of the West Highland Way northwards for several kilometres to take you back towards the lift system access road, while another slightly shorter option (in well frozen conditions) is to head directly East across the edge of Rannoch Moor to reach the A82 at the edge of Loch Ba (Grid Ref: NN308497). Glencoe Ski Patrollers still enjoy telling the tale of one of their members skiing across the frozen lochan on the way to the main road only to break through and sink in up to his armpits. Rather than suffering these two generally flat (and often boggy) exit routes, and with modern ski touring setups becoming more commonplace, a preferable option for many will be to skin back up toward the lifts. Once again route choice for skinning back up is wide open, but a line heading generally North West will take you back towards the edge of the Coire Pollach plateau from where a gentle traverse will take you back towards the top of the Access Chair.

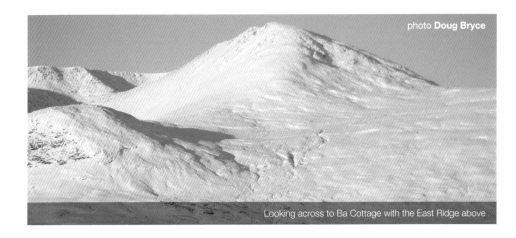

photo **Doug Bryce**

Looking across to Ba Cottage with the East Ridge above

© SkiMountain

Cam Ghleann

The Etive Glades piste is a fantastic run which marks the Western boundary (looker's right) of the ski area and follows the top of the broad North Ridge of Meall a' Bhuiridh. However, as you stray to skier's left of the Etive Glades the hill rolls ominously over into an area of the mountain that has accumulated an altogether more sinister character. This North Western flank of Meall a' Bhuiridh is usually referred to by the name of the glen below – the Cam Ghleann (meaning 'bent glen'). Over the last twenty years, there have been three skier fatalities on this face – two have been caused by slides on ice, while the third was the result of an avalanche in 2013. There has also been at least one very lucky escape from another large avalanche here and as such the area must be respected.

There are a number of factors which make this area of the mountain particularly worthy of caution – firstly, the nature of the large, uniform slope is that it is continuously steep for a substantial distance with a very loose scree and boulder surface underneath, along with a slight convex roll to it; secondly, for almost its entire length this slope terminates in a large cliffed gully feature which is the very definition of a terrain trap; arguably the most significant feature of this slope however, is its proximity to the ski area. Ski Patrol are rightly nervous of skiers straying over in this direction, and the danger signs erected down the ridge pay testament to their preference for you to tread very carefully when considering skiing here. Remember that if you ski over here, others who know less will almost certainly see you and your tracks and may well follow.

Tempting as the skiing in this neck of the woods may be, it is strongly suggested that it should only be skied during very stable (but not icy) conditions. Just because it's close to the lifts, doesn't make it easy, safe, or a good idea.

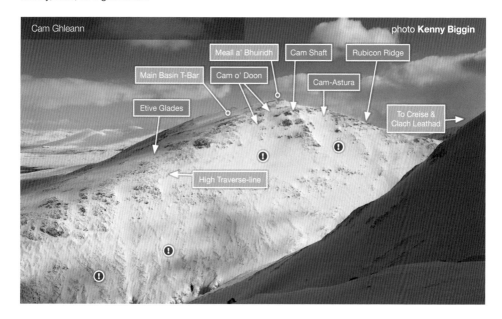

Cam Ghleann — photo **Kenny Biggin**

Meall a' Bhuiridh · Cam Shaft · Rubicon Ridge · Main Basin T-Bar · Cam o' Doon · Cam-Astura · Etive Glades · To Creise & Clach Leathad · High Traverse-line

12. Cam o' Doon

This route can be accessed by traversing across to the Etive Glades from the top of the Main Basin T-bar and dropping over the ridge. Although this route is very easy to get to it is on serious terrain which is treacherous in both icy and unstable conditions.

13. Cam Shaft

On the North West Face directly beneath the summit of Meall a' Bhuiridh there is a small system of vaguely defined gullies between rocks. This can catch the snow and provide good skiing in the right conditions. You can traverse in to the top of it from the top of Etive Glades with a little poling and skating. The lifts make accessing this route easy, but assessing the conditions requires more thought so think carefully before committing yourself onto this potentially dangerous slope.

Spring snow on Cam-Asutra

enny Biggin | rider Blair Fyffe

14. Cam-Asutra

So called because it leaves you in a strange position on the mountain, this is probably the most worthwhile run on this face. If you are sure conditions are safe enough, it can be accessed by either traversing (carefully) from Etive Glades over the top of the Cam Shaft rocks, though better is often to do the short bootpack up onto Meall a' Bhuiridh's summit and descend Rubicon Ridge until you reach a slight flattening. From here there can be good skiing, often in amongst clumps of rocks, and this is one way to ski down into the bottom of Creise Bowl with the aim of skinning up to the ridge on the far side.

Routes Out of the Cam Ghleann

Take care, although right next to the ski area the Cam Ghleann is a serious place

The main feature that dictates where you can and can't ski on this face are the large areas of rocks. When there isn't loads of snow, often the only pitch worth skiing here is the upper couple of hundred metres from where a vague line through the rocks leads back towards the lifts not far from the top of the Wall T-bar. When the face is plastered with enough stable snow (rare) it is possible, though awkward, to ski all the way down towards Camikaze Gorge and do a long traverse at around the 700metre level. This eventually takes you out onto the ridge close to the bottom of the Wall T-bar. More often than not, the snow cover will be patchy at best here, and the steep and rocky nature of the slope makes it a fairly unpleasant experience.

Author's Note on the Cam Ghleann

Please be aware that many local skiers lost a good friend on this part of the hill in 2013. Approach skiing this slope with sensitivity and if in any doubt wait for spring conditions (not ice) and the most stable of NW aspect avalanche reports before venturing this way.

The Cam Ghleann

photo **Neil Muir** | rider **Kenny Biggin**

photo **Kenny Biggin** | rider **Lee Hardy**

Making the most of stable spring conditions in the Cam Ghleann

The South Face

For years many skiers buzzing around on the front of Meall a' Bhuiridh remained largely oblivious to the fact that there was offpiste skiing on offer 'over the back' of the mountain. No doubt some of the in-the-know locals would have liked to keep it that way, but unfortunately (for them) the internet popped that particular balloon some time ago… so secret powder stashes will now have to be sought out that little bit further away. In reality the skiing in this area tends only to be good for short spells of time since the slope faces almost directly South and as such doesn't tend to hold snow, much less good snow, for very long. Although with a big dump of snow there are actually a number of different lines to be taken on this face, including a nice one almost directly from the summit, the three best known lines are described here.

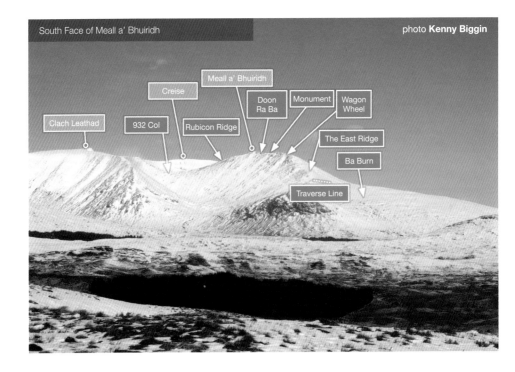

South Face of Meall a' Bhuiridh   photo **Kenny Biggin**

© SkiMountain

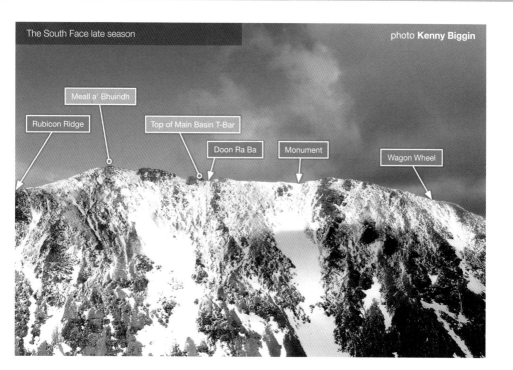

The South Face late season

photo **Kenny Biggin**

Meall a' Bhuiridh

Rubicon Ridge

Top of Main Basin T-Bar

Doon Ra Ba

Monument

Wagon Wheel

15. Doon Ra Ba

2

similar to: Fly Paper

combine with: Ba Cottage

Standing on top of the South Face beside Doon Ra Ba with the top of the T-Bar far left

photo Blair Fyffe

As you take the upper lifts towards the top of the hill it can feel like there are only two options open to you – left or right. In fact, there is a third option awaiting the adventurous – straight on! Get off the t-bar or button to the left and put a few poling skates in to take you past the t-bar's bull wheel and past the concrete lifties' bunker. Once here it becomes obvious that there is a rolling entrance to an inviting gully line with a rocky buttress on skier's right. It should be reasonably easy to tell from here whether there will be enough snow on the face to make this worthwhile – remember that there will also need to be enough snow to traverse out to the left around halfway down the face.

skimountain

Charlie Kennedy's monument beside his path across to the Spring Run from the T-Bar

photo **Kenny Biggin**

16. Monument

similar to: Doon Ra Ba

Further along the South Face to skier's left, there is another similar line that can give great skiing. You can find the top of the route by following the walled path along towards the Spring Run until you get to a cairn with a plaque on it on your right. This is a memorial to Charlie Kennedy who spent a summer building the traverse from the main basin over to the Spring Run and Fly Paper. In good snow years it is sometimes possible to ski all the way down to the lochan. If there is so much snow that you think the cairn may be buried, the entrance to this gully can be found by skating along the edge from Doon Ra Ba for a short way.

17. Wagon Wheel

| similar to: | Monument |

Still further along the South Face is a run called Wagon Wheel. The entrance to this is found by following the walled path along past the Charlie Kennedy monument as far as the top of the Spring Run. From here turn right and skate up to the edge of the ridge. The run drops down the South Face between bands of rock in a similar fashion to Monument and Doon Ra Ba, with great views of Clach Leathad opposite. After a couple of hundred metres of descent, hang a left with the aim of joining the lower section of the East Ridge.

Glencoe folklore tells that the run was nicknamed Wagon Wheel (by Bruce and Eric Thomson) after the balls of wet snow that often cartwheel down this south facing steep slope when they skied it for the first time in the 1980s.

Andy Meldrum checking out his backyard at the top of Monument

photo Kenny Biggin | rider Andy Meldrum

GLENCOE

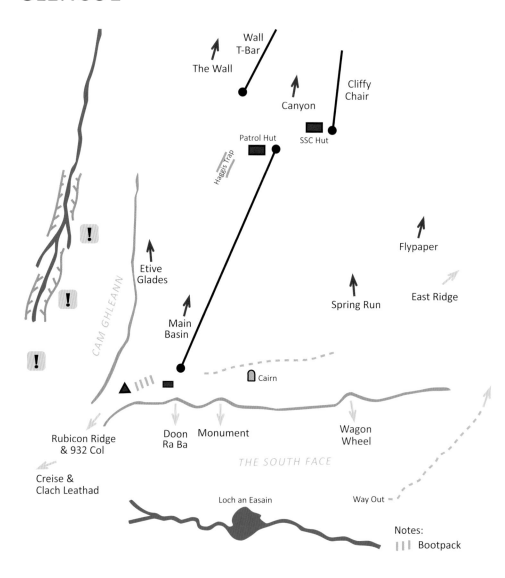

Wall
T-Bar

The Wall

Canyon

Cliffy
Chair

Patrol Hut

SSC Hut

Haggis Trap

Etive
Glades

Flypaper

CAM GHLEANN

Spring Run

East Ridge

Main
Basin

Cairn

Rubicon Ridge
& 932 Col

Doon
Ra Ba

Monument

Wagon
Wheel

THE SOUTH FACE

Creise &
Clach Leathad

Way Out

Loch an Easain

Notes:

||| Bootpack

© SkiMountain

Traversing out from the South Face

photo B... ...

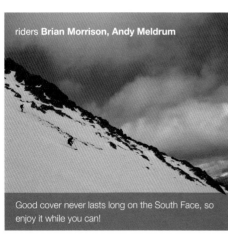

riders **Brian Morrison, Andy Meldrum**

Good cover never lasts long on the South Face, so enjoy it while you can!

photo **Kenny Biggin** | rider **Dave Biggin**

Arriving back at the ski area after a South Face foray

▲skimountain

Beyond Meall a' Bhuiridh

Wait until there is a good covering of snow and a nice sunny day, take the lifts up to the top, get off the Main Basin T-bar on the right hand side and do a short bootpack up to the summit of Meall a' Bhuiridh. What you will see spread out in front of you is Glencoe Mountain Resort's very own backcountry skiing mecca. Connected to Meall a' Bhuiridh by a kilometre long ridge (Rubicon Ridge), there are two fantastic mountains within relatively easy reach of the lifts – Clach Leathad lies to the left with Creise on the right. It should go without saying that heading across to these mountains you are leaving the ski resort behind and taking responsibility for yourself – there are all the usual risks of heading into the backcountry, not least avalanche risk, slips on ice, cliffs, adverse weather, navigation mistakes, etc. – try hard to avoid getting into trouble and be prepared.

18. Rubicon Ridge

harder than:	East Ridge
combine with:	Loch an Easain, Creise and Clach Leathad

Strong winds at the 932 Col with Rubicon Ridge behind

photo **Kenny Biggin** | rider Neil

© SkiMountain

Leading off the summit of Meall a' Bhuiridh to the South West, there is a rocky ridge heading down to 932 Col (at 932metres) before rising up to Creise and Clach Leathad. The ridge can't really be described as broad, but nor is it particularly steep or narrow – when there is a good covering of snow the ski down the ridge itself can be worth a trip in its own right. Very often the ridge doesn't hold snow well and in these conditions going down it becomes a means to an end - getting to 932 Col is likely to involve some walking over awkward rocks, however it isn't too far so is often worth it to access the good skiing on the hills beyond.

If the ridge itself has no snow on it, it is often possible to link various snowfields together on the slope to the right (Cam-Asutra) – either heading back to 932 Col or a nicer line can be to make a bee line for a point lower than the col in the bowl below Creise from where an easy skin will take you back to the ridge. Tread very carefully here as the slope to the right is notorious with a large terrain trap below so should only be used in stable conditions (see section on the Cam Ghleann).

Author's Note: The Rubicon is a river in Italy - crossing the Rubicon means to pass a point of no return, and comes from Julius Caesar leading his army across the river in 49 BC. It's not quite a point of no return, but by going down this ridge you are very definitely heading away from the lifts and into the backcountry – have fun!

Unusual amounts of snow on Rubicon Ridge

photo **Dave Biggin** | rider **Kenny Biggin**

19. Loch an Easain

combine with: Rubicon Ridge

From 932 Col at the bottom of Rubicon Ridge, a relatively easy offpiste route leads down to the South East into the large basin below Clach Leathad that holds the picturesque Loch an Easain. When there is plenty of snow (and if you don't mind the slightly awkward ski down Rubicon Ridge) this is an adventurous route that will introduce you to the geography of Glencoe's backcountry without committing to skiing anything too steep. Dropping off the col, pick the line that is holding the most snow and roughly follow the burn line all the way down towards the lochan, sticking to the left bank as you get closer towards it. Continue traversing up above the lochan on the left, with the South Face routes of Meall a' Bhuiridh up above you, and aim to get roughly to just above the col at the bottom of the East Ridge. From here you can do a poling traverse back round towards the lifts. Depending how low you drop and how amenable the snowpack is, you may need to bootpack or skin back up a couple of hundred metres – bear in mind that the lochan is at 630metres, while the bottom of the Plateau Button is at around 670metres.

With low lying snow, and for those feeling fit, it is also possible to follow the Allt Coire an Easain down below the lochan, continuing all the way down towards where the gradient flattens out and leads to the River Ba. This is a fantastic remote feeling yet easy route but it leaves you some distance away from civilisation – the way out from here is to either skin back up the way you have come, or traverse out towards Ba Cottage and then skin back to the lifts from there.

GERMAN ENGINEERED
SINCE 1898

PACKS DESIGNED FOR SNOW & BUILT TO LAST

DEUTERGB.CO.UK

Creise

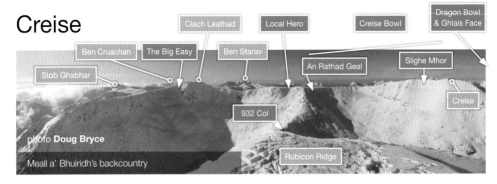

Ben Cruachan · The Big Easy · Clach Leathad · Ben Starav · Local Hero · Creise Bowl · Dragon Bowl & Ghlais Face · Stob Ghabhar · An Rathad Geal · Slighe Mhor · Creise · 932 Col · Rubicon Ridge

photo **Doug Bryce**

Meall a' Bhuiridh's backcountry

As you drive across the River Etive and past the Kingshouse towards Glencoe Mountain Resort from the North, you get a fantastic view into the bowls and faces of Creise. This mountain is a real jewel for Glencoe skiers and good tracks on its flanks are highly prized amongst locals. Despite the fact that you get a great view of Creise's main bowls from the Etive Glades and the Plateau area of the lifts, relatively few skiers make the journey across. For those that do venture in this direction and find good snow, pick your line well and make your turns count - the tracks will be there for all to see.

Creise has three main areas of interest to the offpiste skier – the first two are large bowls referred to here as the Creise Bowl, and the Dragon Bowl, each of which contain a variety of lines and routes suitable for most tastes. The third area is less visible from the lifts and drops down the North East Face of Stob a' Ghlais Choire.

Looking across to Creise from Plateau Poma with Dragon Bowl upper left and The Ghlais Face on the right above the Café

photo Kenny Biggin

© SkiMountain

photo **Kenny Biggin**

Creise

Creise Bowl

Rubicon Ridge

Local Hero

Slighe Mhor

Clach Leathad

Wickerman

Slighe Bheag

An Rathad Geal

932 Col

Access

Access to Creise can be attained relatively easily by using the lifts to take you up to the top, and then a short bootpack to the summit of Meall a' Bhuiridh takes you to the start of Rubicon Ridge (see route description in previous section). Once at 932 Col at Grid Ref: NN243501, the ridge leads up onto a flat plateau with Creise to the right and Clach Leathad to the left. The ridge up onto the plateau is fairly gentle for most of its length and is an easy angle to skin or walk up. Only the last 50metres is a bit steeper and care should be taken here – it can be necessary to stop and get crampons and axe out just to get up the last 20 steps: sometimes frustrating but necessary. Late in the season there will often be little snow left on the ridge and at this time of year it can make sense to wear walking boots or trainers to get all the way across and change back into your ski boots at the top of your chosen line.

CREISE

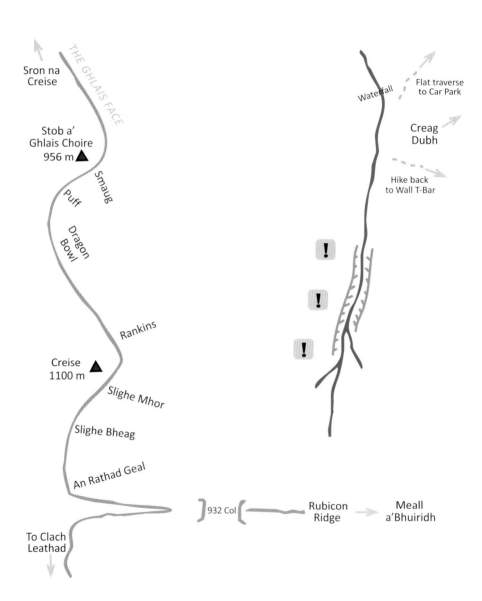

Sron na
Creise

THE GHLAIS FACE

Stob a'
Ghlais Choire
956 m ▲

Puff

Smaug

Dragon
Bowl

Rankins

Creise ▲
1100 m

Slighe Mhor

Slighe Bheag

An Rathad Geal

To Clach
Leathad

932 Col

Rubicon
Ridge

Meall
a'Bhuiridh

Waterfall

Flat traverse
to Car Park

Creag
Dubh

Hike back
to Wall T-Bar

20. Creise and Back

combine with: Clach Leathad & Back / Creise Bowl

Sometimes you don't want to ski epic long descents or knee deep powder, and on these occasions perhaps the thing to do is go on a journey instead. Going across to Creise and back from Meall a' Bhuiridh is a great way to suss out the lay of the land at the same time as getting away from the crowds for a while and making use of all that shiny new touring kit you've just bought yourself. Head down Meall a' Bhuiridh's Rubicon Ridge and skin up the other side as far as possible. Clamber up onto the plateau as best you can and then enjoy the tour along the flattish plateau to Creise's summit. The way back for this route is to retrace your steps, with the only real difficulty being the first few turns going back down onto the ridge. Usually it is reasonably easy to ski back onto the ridge if you slide in a little to the left.

Rubicon Ridge leading back up to Meall a' Bhuiridh is often too rocky or awkward to skin up, so popping your skis on your back may be the way forward. Enjoy the solitude for as long as you can as you climb back up the ridge, as the hordes will be waiting beyond.

21. Creise Bowl

similar to: Fly Paper

Lying immediately to the right of the ridge leading from Meall a' Bhuiridh lies a large open bowl known here simply as the Creise Bowl. There are a myriad of nice lines into this bowl with no real definition between them – the main choice will be dictated by where the snow is lying and how the cornices have formed in any particular season. The skiing in general in this bowl is relatively open and easy, although with the large terrain trap of the Cam Ghleann gulch lying somewhere down below, skiers should always wait for stable conditions before skiing here.

Access the bowl by climbing up the ridge from Meall a' Bhuiridh in whatever fashion conditions dictate, and then pick your way into the bowl wherever you choose. There are three particularly nice lines here – the first lies directly beside the access ridge and has been called An Rathad Geal (The White Road) because it faces North East and at the end of the season snow lingers here and often presents a persistent strip of white leading down into the corrie. In the middle of the bowl, Slighe Bheag (pronounced 'slee-uh vake', meaning simply Little Route) provides good skiing provided there

You can still have a good day if you forget your salopettes - dropping into Slighe Mhor in jeans in Creise Bowl.

is enough snow to fill in the easier lines between the rocks. At the far end of the bowl lies Slighe Mhòr ('slee-uh vore' - the Big Route) which is a fine, long line coming down almost straight off the summit of Creise – this is probably the most commonly skied line on Creise and snow seems to collect well here.

Once down in the bottom of the bowl, there are a choice of exit strategies – which to go for will largely depend on how the snow is lying. The main choices are to teeter your way along the flank above the Cam Ghleann gulch (see the section on the Cam Ghleann for more on this), or the safer option is usually to skin back up to 932 Col and back up the Rubicon Ridge.

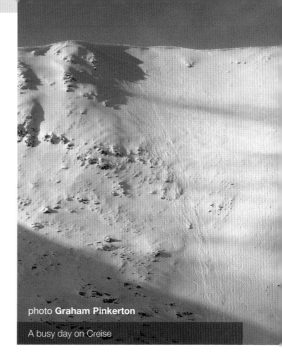

photo **Graham Pinkerton**

A busy day on Creise

Author's Note: The OS 1:25,000 map marks this corrie as Mam Coire Easain. Sometimes 'mam' is used to refer to a rounded hill, which could refer to the indistinct bump on the ridge in between Creise and Clach Leathad, however in this context it seems more likely that the name has been put in the wrong place over the years and the name may actually refer to the col (932 Col) at the base of Rubicon Ridge – 'Mam Coire Easain' = 'The bealach of the corrie with the small waterfall'.

22. Rankins

harder than: Dragon Bowl

This line drops directly off the broad summit down the North Face to skier's left of the loosely defined North East Ridge of Creise. Although it is really just the far edge of the Dragon Bowl it tends to have quite differing snow conditions (and can sometimes be quite scoured). It is a classy line and probably the most aesthetically pure of these top two bowls of Creise. It is named after Philip Rankin who was the main man behind getting Scotland's first lift system going at Glencoe way back in 1956.

23. The Dragon

harder than:	Creag Dhubh Chute
combine with:	Dragon Bowl

From a certain angle the rocky cliffs at the summit of Stob a' Ghlais Choire have been said to look like a Dragon (have a look and make your own mind up). Cutting down through these distinctive crags that make up the Northern end of the bowl, there are two tight slot like gullies. Both are fairly short and only sometimes fill with enough snow to be good options for skiing, however they are quite iconic features of this face and as such are well worth a look when in condition. As befitting these short but fiery lines, they have been named after famous dragons - the skier's right line, 'Puff', is more open and generally more friendly, but often less snowy. The skier's left line - 'Smaug' - is a menacing steep and narrow gully with a dogleg around two thirds of the way down it – a lot of snow is required for the top section to be skiable, and unwary skiers are likely to get burnt.

The Dragon, with the lines of Puff on the left and Smaug with the dogleg on the right

photo **Kenny Biggin**

Dropping into the Dragon Bowl with 'The Dragon' behind

photo Kenny Biggin | rider **Neil Muir**

24. The Dragon Bowl

similar to: Creise Bowl

In between the summits of Creise and Stob a' Ghlais Choire lies a large and open bowl with the distinctive set of crags (The Dragon) at its Northern end. The corrie gets its Gaelic name (Glas Choire) from the grey appearance of the rocks. As with Creise Bowl, it is possible to ski many different lines into this bowl, and which you choose will depend on your taste for cornices, fresh tracks, and of course consideration about which aspect will be best and safest. Usually the easiest entrance will be reached by skiing off the summit of Creise down to the low point on the ridge before you get to the crags at the far end.

For those (sensible people) who don't wish to get too close to the Cam Ghleann gulch which lies below, it is best to stop in the bottom of the main bowl at an obvious flattening before going over the next rise. From here a good option is often to skin back up for another run, but if you're heading back to the lifts it is best to traverse out left towards the broad ridge until you are past the worst part of the gorge down below. Then ski down to a spot that looks good for crossing the burn and either traverse round the side of Creag Dhubh and back to the access car park, or skin or hike back up to the col that takes you out at the bottom of the Etive Glades and so to the bottom of The Wall T-bar. In the right conditions it can also be possible to traverse out high to skier's right in order to cut across the top of the Cam Ghleann gulch and from there back to the lifts (but note warnings elsewhere about crossing this slope).

25. The Ghlais Face

harder than: Dragon Bowl

The Northern-most summit of Creise is called Stob a' Ghlais Choire at a height of 996metres. This peak has the ridge of Sron na Creise to its North and the Dragon Bowl to the South. Tucked away on the North East Face there are some spectacular lines that you can see in all their glory from the main road close to the Kingshouse. There are multiple different routes which you can take down this face, with ribs of rock separating mainly open gully lines. The most obvious line is found by skiing off the summit in a North Easterly direction for around 200metres before approaching the edge and taking a look over. From the Kingshouse this face looks much steeper than it actually is, but this is perfect avalanche terrain so keep your wits about you. There are six main lines on the face (plus the couloir described separately below) and these have picked up the following eclectic names, starting on skier's right: Boonies, Weegies, The Lair (of the Slabbybogle!), Wonderland (the usual line), Skinny Malinky, and on the far side of the couloir, Sassenachs. The two lines either side of the Ghlais Couloir are noticeably trickier than the others although they are all roughly similar in character.

The upper reaches of this face tend to catch and hold snow reasonably well, although the best time to ski it is when there is snow down to car park level. In these conditions it is possible to get a great run of around 500metres of fairly consistent gradient. Once past the steeper part of the face, the best route is to trend to skier's right, aiming for a flat and bouldery part of the Allt Cam Ghlinne some way downstream of an obvious waterfall, where it is usually reasonably easy to cross (so long as it isn't in spate!). From here you can hike or skin back up to the col next to Creag Dhubh from where you can get back to the bottom of the Wall T-bar. Alternatively it is often just as easy to traverse around the bottom of the North West Ridge of Creag Dhubh and then endure the 1½km flat and boggy, but not too taxing trudge back to the car park.

Stob a' Ghlais Choire

The Ghlais Face

photo **Kenny Biggin**

Wonderland

Skinny Malinky

Ghlais Couloir

Sassenachs

Sron na Creise

Creise

Weegies

The Lair

Rankins

Boonies

The Ghlais Face at its best

Author's Note: In some editions of the climbing guides there are routes on this face, with the main line being the Inglis Clarke Ridge (Grade III) which lies in between Wonderland and Skinny Malinky. The gullies are sometimes named with numbers from left to right (Wonderland is Gully 4), but the names used here are hoped to be more engaging. You can also have a great ski in the right conditions by following the broad ridge line that leads down in between the Ghlais Face and Dragon Bowl, though this is often overlooked in favour of the classier routes on either side – if doing multiple laps, this ridge can offer a good way to skin back up.

26. Ghlais Couloir

harder than: Wonderland, Creag Dhubh Chute

Although most of the lines on Stob a' Ghlais Choire's North East Face are reasonably open, there is also an impressive narrow couloir feature which lies to skier's left of the face. In a snowy year this provides inspiration and temptation to skiers looking for a challenge. The feature has picked up several different names over the years, with some climbers knowing it variously as Central / Broad Gully or the imaginative 'Gully 6'. Around 2008 the feature also picked up the name Bad Boy Gully (or Bad Boy Creise) when it was skied by Doug and Ally Paton, and Hamish MacEwan.

Whatever you call it, the gully is a great skiing objective. The pitch is steep but not ridiculously so, while the almost inevitably corniced entrance and rock walls towering up on both sides provide a real atmosphere and of course a perfect photo opportunity. Once out of the main couloir, continue down the face and pick up the route description for the Ghlais Face.

Late season turns in the Ghlais Couloir

photo **Blair Aitken** | rider **Kenny Biggin**

Tight turns in the Ghlais Couloir

photo **Kenny Biggin** | rider **Blair Aitken**

Further down the Cam Ghleann after skiing the Ghlais Face

Tickling the Dragon – looking down Puff

photo **Neil Muir** | rider **Kenny Biggin**

Dragon Bowl - Yes, Scottish skiing really can be this good!

Neil taking a look through the looking-glass into Wonderland

photo **Kenny Biggin** | rider **Neil Muir**

The Slabbybogle

(Written by Kenny while reflecting on a close encounter with an avalanche on the Ghlais Face. A 'bogle' is a Scots word for a ghost or other scary creature – the Slabbybogle's better known cousin is the Tattybogle… a scarecrow.)

Beware the fearsome Slabbybogle, Freeriders of Glencoe,
On the Black Mount and Ben Lui, They sought it high and low,
They searched around the Buachailles, And even on Ben Do',
And on the flanks of Sgreamhach, Adorned in pristine snow,
And everywhere they searched and looked, No matter how they tried,
To second guess the sneaky fiend, The 'Bogle skipped aside.

On Bidean they thought they'd found it, But alas they were too slow,
The 'Bogle it had moved its lair, The trickster of a foe,
They tried to learn its ways and means, And where it meant to go,
But it snuck off to the shadows, With beady eyes still all a-glow,
Which is when they let their guard down, And thought it justified,
To venture one step further, For that tempting offpiste ride.

And so they came to venture forth, Beyond the back of 'Bhuiridh,
Across to Creise's fine Ghlais Face, Unaware the lurking fury,
Just one small step is all it took, To wake the 'Bogle's slumber,
Despite all those years of careful toil, The 'Bogle had their number.

So please take heed this warning, Freeriders please beware,
You may think yourself an expert … But the Slabbybogle doesn't care!

Clach Leathad

Ah, Clach Leathad... apart from the problem of knowing how to pronounce it (roughly Clach-let) this fantastic mountain is perfectly situated for Glencoe skiers – it is just far enough away from the lifts to keep the numbers down, but just close enough to make skiing it pretty achievable. From the front of the ski resort you could easily remain completely oblivious that this peak was even there, however if you take the trouble of doing the short bootpack to the summit of Meall a' Bhuiridh or even just ski to the top of one of the South Face runs like Doon Ra Ba or Monument, you are presented with the impressive sight of a large steep bowl with plenty of options for the discerning backcountry skier.

Access

The route across to Clach Leathad is the same as for Creise – usually this will involve skiing or walking down Meall a' Bhuiridh's Rubicon Ridge to 932 Col followed by a short skin or bootpack up onto the plateau. Sometimes crampons and axe are required to get up the last little bit of the ridge, so come prepared.

photo **Kenny Biggin**

Forsair Rib
Easain Chute
The Skoosh
Pig Leathad
The Big Easy
Clach Leathad

© SkiMountain

Sron nam Forsair | Forsair Bowl | Forsair Rib | Easain Chute | The Big Easy | Clach Leathad

photo **Kenny Biggin**

photo **Kenny Biggin**

The Big Easy | Clach Leathad | Wickerman | Local Hero | Creise

Pig Leathad

932 Col

Rubicon Ridge

CLACH LEATHAD

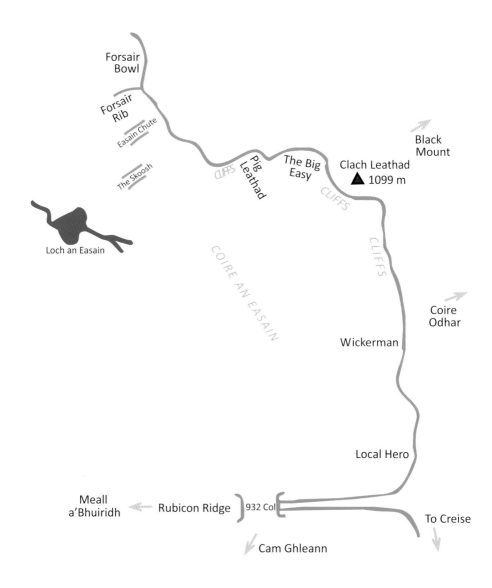

Forsair
Bowl

Forsair
Rib

Easain Chute

The Skoosh

CLIFFS

Pig
Leathad

The Big
Easy

Clach Leathad
▲ 1099 m

Black
Mount

CLIFFS

CLIFFS

Loch an Easain

COIRE AN EASAIN

Coire
Odhar

Wickerman

Local Hero

Meall
a'Bhuiridh

Rubicon Ridge

932 Col

To Creise

Cam Ghleann

27. Clach Leathad & Back

similar to: Creise & Back

combine with: Local Hero, Loch an Easain

For those who don't fancy dropping into the steep bowl, or for those who just want a jaunt in the mountains, heading over the top of Meall a' Bhuiridh and over to Clach Leathad and back can be the perfect remedy. Although it is sometimes possible to ski down the Rubicon Ridge from the ski hill, more often than not this is fairly rocky and will require at least some walking. Skinning up the far side to the plateau can be rewarding though, as once up there are fantastic views (weather permitting) over the Black Mount and beyond to the Glen Etive hills such as Ben Starav.

From the top of the connecting ridge, turn left onto the plateau and continue across mellow terrain before a gentle rise takes you on up to the summit of Clach Leathad. When not buried by snow (as it was in 2014), the summit has a comprehensive windbreak that offers a great place for a sandwich and a cuppa before heading back the way you came. The only steeper skiing involved in this excursion is getting back down onto the ridge to link back to Meall a' Bhuiridh. There is usually a slightly easier entrance just to the North (skier's left) side of the ridge, and of course you should have had a good look at your route when you were on your way across. Much of the time re-ascending Meall a' Bhuiridh via the Rubicon Ridge will be the best choice, however it is worth noting that in certain snow conditions it is possible from 932 Col to traverse all the way across the South Face, picking your way between the rocks, until you pick up the bottom of the East Ridge.

photo **David Shortt** | rider **Kenny Biggin**

Peering into Local Hero

 **skimountain**

28. Local Hero

harder than: Creise Bowl

As you are topping out on the ridge coming across from the ski hill, the first skiable line on Clach Leathad lies immediately to the South. There is a mini bowl here between the small crag at the top of the ridge and the next outcrop. This line offers two possibilities – you can either drop in and ski pretty much all the way down to the lochan, or you can ski the top few hundred feet and then break out to skier's left to head back to 932 Col. Although this line is quite open, the top pitch is actually fairly steep and rocky so wait for good snow.

29. Wickerman

harder than: Local Hero

Further along the corrie to the South of Local Hero leading round to the summit of Clach Leathad, there is a large selection of steep cliffs that frequently exhibit large cornices. The exact routes that are possible beside (or perhaps even in amongst) the cliffs depend on how well the snow has built up around the scarp wall. In some years there is little skiable here, but in snowy winters the part of the

Tricky to get to the edge at Wickerman with Clach Leathad and The Big Easy behind

photo **Kenny Biggin**

bowl on skier's left usually fills in and provides brilliant skiing. Because of the shape of the bowl, it can be very tricky getting to the edge here for a look without standing blindly on top of cornices. You can usually get a good look at the lines from the ridge on the way up, but once up close there are few if any opportunities to pick a spot without gambling going out to the edge. Best either to ski Local Hero first and look back up, or you can sometimes sneak a look into the bowl from the prow at the far skier's left of the bowl.

Note that the easiest lines here usually lie a fair way before you get to the shallow col on the way to Clach Leathad – by the time you get to the col you are above cliffs. There is also a rarely skied line to skier's left of the summit cliffs, but snow cover is unreliable here and cornices are frequently prohibitive.

30. Coire Odhar

similar to:	Spring Run
combine with:	Forsair Rib

When going along the flat plateau that leads to the summit of Clach Leathad, you can drop down to the West into Coire Odhar. Since the corrie is largely West facing and the prevailing wind comes from the South West, there tends to be less consistent snow here than on the North East faces. Having said that, the top of the bowl frequently does have enough snow to give good skiing and in the right conditions there is some nice open, and not too steep, bowl skiing here. Usually, it will be a case of skiing the top two or three hundred metres and then skinning back up, potentially making a loop of it

Mellow skiing in Coire Odhar

photo **Kenny Biggin**

by skinning up the curved ridge that leads up to Clach Leathad's summit. Once in a while however (for the adventurous amongst you) the option of skiing all the way down to Glen Etive becomes a possibility.

The run all the way down to Glen Etive is probably the longest vertical descent in this book (1000metres of descent), but enough snow down to just above sea level to make this route worthwhile is a rare occurrence. What's more there is a long (3km) and fairly flat ski out once the angle eases off (not fun in deep soft snow), so this should be seen as more of an expedition into the boonies as much as anything else. If you do decide to explore in this direction note that you should leave a car in advance down Glen Etive at the bridge (Grid Ref: NN198513) across the River Etive just upstream of the confluence with the Allt a' Chaorainn (a spot well known to the white water kayakers amongst you).

Other escapades down off the hills towards Glen Etive might also seem like a good idea, but note that the bridge mentioned here is the only easy way across the river.

31. The Big Easy

harder than: Local Hero, Rankins

Perhaps the most striking line on Clach Leathad is its North East Face. Directly underneath the summit there is a line of large black cliffs, but to skier's right of these it is possible to drop into a large open bowl / face with around 400metres of nice descent before you get to the lochan. The route in gets easier the further from the summit you go, but dropping in right beside the edge of the cliffs gives the longest run and is steep enough to make most people pause for thought. This is one of those lines that is well worth trying to catch in condition so that forever more you'll be able to glance across and think "I've skied that".

Pig Leathad feeling steep in the mist

photo **Kenny Biggin** | rider **Lee Hardy**

32. Pig Leathad

4 ⚠ ⚠

harder than: Easain Chute, The Big Easy

Beyond the main North East Face there are a series of rocky ribs with a couple of short gullies of varying degrees of difficulty in between. The most skiable of these are the first two and they make exciting alternatives to skiing the main face. Both of these lines are steep enough to mean jump turns are likely to be needed, but both have enough width to give you a bit of room to breath. In some snow conditions a third gully option opens up but this is generally steeper, narrower, and rockier.

⚠ skimountain

photo **Kenny Biggin** | rider **David Shortt**

33. Easain Chute

3

harder than: Forsair Rib

When looking across at Clach Leathad from the summit of Meall a' Bhuiridh, the Easain Chute is an obvious gully line which cuts through the cliffs almost directly above the lochan around half a kilometre down the ridge from the summit. This is a very pleasing line to ski, but be warned that it gets very little sun so can remain rock hard when snow all around has softened. Finding the entrance can be tricky since you can't see the whole way down it from the top. Skiing from the summit, keep going until the ridge turns an obvious corner – from this point the gully entrance lies around 2-300 metres further on. If you get to the point where the ridge starts dropping away you have gone too far. You have to take a leap of faith at the top and ski the first few turns before being able to see down the gully itself, and here the entrance rolls over slightly into a steepening which can be a little disconcerting. In nice snow this is a great run and not too difficult... but not a nice place to be on ice.

34. The Skoosh

combine with: Easain Chute, The Big Easy

This gully like feature lies on the lower slopes of the corrie in between The Big Easy and the Easain Chute and makes an exciting end to those routes. The gully can feel fairly steep in its own right, and seeing avi debris here is not uncommon.

35. Forsair Rib

similar to: Dragon Bowl

harder than: Forsair Bowl

Marking the end of the main North and Eastern corries of Clach Leathad, this route drops down towards the lochan from Clach Leathad's East Ridge before it starts dropping away to the East. You can find the route by skiing from the summit, past the obvious bend in the ridge, and keep going for around half a kilometre. The ridge starts to descend at this point but it is possible to drop left onto a broad shoulder or rib that takes you Northwards down towards the lochan. There is more than one way down here and you can either cut back to skier's left through a gap in the rocks or continue down the broad rib itself. Either way, this route makes an easier (though no less rewarding) way off the mountain and is a good option for those who've decided the routes higher up are not for them.

photo **Kenny Biggin** | rider **Lee Hardy**

Shelter from the storm on the summit of Clach Leathad

Looking across to Clach Leathad with Meall a' Bhuiridh's East Ridge on the right

36. Sron nam Forsair & Forsair Bowl

similar to: East Ridge

For those who enjoy skiing the East Ridge of Meall a' Bhuiridh, you may also have looked across and thought about skiing its sister route – the East Ridge of Clach Leathad or Sron nam Forsair to give it its proper name. Good conditions are reasonably infrequent to stay on the ridge the whole way down (and the slope actually drops away fairly steeply in the wrong direction to the South). The route that usually works quite nicely though, is to descend the ridge until you are just above the prominent bump or 'nose' that gives it its name, and then drop into a minor bowl that sits to skier's right of the Forsair Rib. The Forsair Bowl heads off to the North East, and there is some great skiing here at a reasonably easy angle. The only thing about this route is that it starts taking you away from the lochan and the usual route out, but it is a great adventure. For those feeling the urge to do something different you should give it a shot – keep skiing down here until you run out of snow, find a way across the burn, and then skin back towards the ski hill.

Route Out from Coire an Easain

The majority of the routes above take you down towards Loch an Easain. This lochan lies underneath the South Face of Meall a' Bhuiridh and can also be skied to via routes such as Doon Ra Ba and Monument. If the snow cover isn't great, then for some of the routes higher up such as Local Hero and Wickerman, it can be best to cut out left reasonably high and make for 932 Col and Meall a' Bhuiridh's Rubicon Ridge as a way back to the ski hill. Most of the time though, it makes sense just to accept the inevitable and enjoy the ski all the way to the lochan. There is some steep ground on these lower slopes so pick your route carefully trying to link together as much snow as you can while avoiding the nastier looking slabs of rock.

Once at the lochan it is best to cross over the burn a little upstream of it before starting to contour round the side in an Easterly direction. With enough snow it is worth putting skins on here and a twenty minute skin usually takes you back round to the traverse line near the bottom of the East Ridge. If there isn't much snow, hike round onto the bottom of the broad East Ridge and pick your way back round to the ski hill. It is usually worth bootpacking up the ridge to around 800metres as from here it is often possible to get your skis back on and do a skating traverse back towards the lifts.

Spring snow on the Forsair Rib with the remnants of Doon Ra Ba and Monument on the slope behind

photo **Kenny Biggin** | rider **David Shortt**

The Black Mount

No book about skiing in Glencoe would be complete without describing the Black Mount. This is an area which lies to the South of the ski hill stretching from Meall a' Bhuiridh, over Creise and Clach Leathad, to Stob Ghabhar and Stob a' Choire Odhair which lie above Victoria Bridge, near Bridge of Orchy.

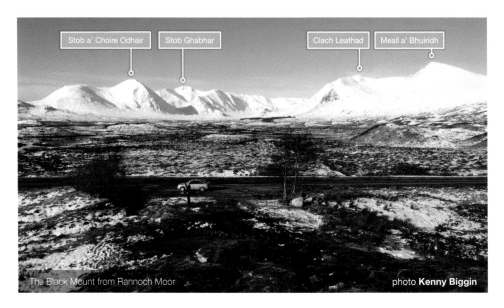

Stob a' Choire Odhair Stob Ghabhar Clach Leathad Meall a' Bhuiridh

The Black Mount from Rannoch Moor   photo **Kenny Biggin**

37. The Black Mount Traverse

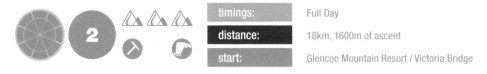

timings:	Full Day
distance:	18km, 1600m of ascent
start:	Glencoe Mountain Resort / Victoria Bridge

This ski tour is a real Glencoe classic and comes highly prized as getting it in good conditions is a fine art that relatively few teams have succeeded in pulling off. The traverse has the Glencoe Mountain Resort lift system at one end and Victoria Bridge near Bridge of Orchy at the other. It is equally possible to do the traverse in either direction, although there seems to be a slight preference to go from South to North. There are pros and cons of each direction – starting at the North end means you can use the lifts to take you to the top of Meall a' Bhuiridh (so long as they open early enough for your alpine start regime), but in prevailing weather the snow is more likely to be better for the descents when going South to North. There is something nice about finishing by skiing down beside the lifts after they've closed and arriving just in time for a well-earned pint at Café Ossian, so the route is described here starting at Victoria Bridge.

BLACK MOUNT

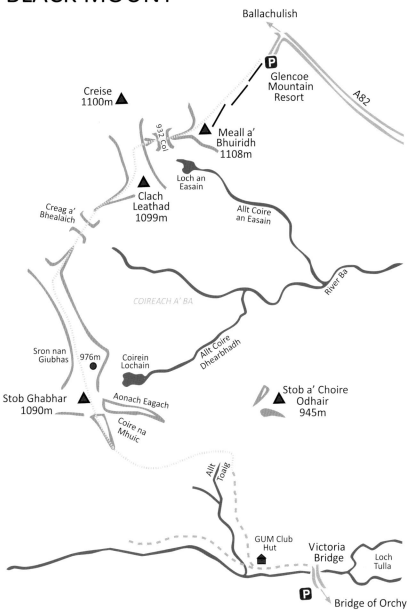

Ballachulish

Glencoe
Mountain
Resort

A82

Creise
1100m

932 Col

Meall a'
Bhuiridh
1108m

Loch an
Easain

Clach
Leathad
1099m

Creag a'
Bhealaich

Allt Coire
an Easain

River Ba

COIREACH A' BA

Allt Coire
Dhearbhadh

Sron nan
Giubhas

976m

Coirein
Lochain

Stob a' Choire
Odhair
945m

Stob Ghabhar
1090m

Aonach Eagach

Coire na
Mhuic

Allt
Toaig

GUM Club
Hut

Victoria
Bridge

Loch
Tulla

Bridge of Orchy

After leaving a shuttle car at the ski area car park, pull off the A82 at Bridge of Orchy and follow the single track road up to Victoria Bridge. Park your car at the designated parking area and sort your kit out (light is right!). Follow the road over the bridge and then turn left onto the track that takes you along beside the river to Clashgour. Here there is a small green hut which started out life as a four pupil primary school but is now known as the GUM Club hut since it is owned by Glasgow University Mountaineering Club.

From the hut turn right onto a rough path that follows the Allt Toaig. In snowy conditions you may even have your skins on by now, but often you will have to walk a fair way up before taking your skis off your back. Since the path up the Allt Toaig is actually quite good higher up, it is worth following it until you are at around 500metres high. At this point, strike out West across the base of the Aonach Eagach ridge and traverse across the lower reaches of Coire na Muic (note it's not THE Aonach Eagach). Aim to get up on to Stob Ghabhar's broad South Ridge at around Grid Ref: NN237445. Follow the ridge up all the way to the summit, taking time to appreciate the spectacular East Face of Stob Ghabhar and the views all around.

Having spent a few minutes patting yourself on the back for getting to the top of Stob Ghabhar – an achievement in its own right – it is time to make a decision about whether to commit to doing the whole traverse. If the weather is bad or if party members are flagging, now is the time to turn back – there are some excellent skiing possibilities dropping back to the South East into Coire na Muic. Should you decide to continue, ski off the summit towards the North where a gentle but enjoyable slope lies waiting to reward your efforts so far. Keep your speed up to slide as far as you can across the long flat plateau past Sron nan Giubhas and towards Aonach Mor. There are a number of undulations on this ridge and putting skins back on here is usually worthwhile. Finding the correct point to turn right off the ridge is a key piece of navigation, so keep your wits about you here. The ridge across to Clach Leathad drops off the plateau at around Grid Ref: NN224477.

Another short pitch of descent takes you down to Creag a' Bhealaich and from here it's skins on again to climb the fairly steep South Easterly flank of Clach Leathad. No doubt legs will be getting tired by the time the summit of Clach Leathad is reached, but from here you are entering the finishing straight. If you're not fussed about completing the traverse, you could choose to ski off Clach Leathad via The Big Easy or another route from here, but the purists will descend along the ridge / plateau towards Creise and drop down onto Meall a' Bhuiridh's Rubicon Ridge. This is potentially the most technical portion of the whole trip, so care should be taken to find the right spot (roughly Grid Ref: NN238500).

Either traverse from 932 Col all the way across the South Face, or ski, climb, or skin back up the Rubicon Ridge to the summit of Meall a'Bhuiridh and take a moment to enjoy the setting sun and deserted pistes, before putting your legs through one last long descent to get down to the car park.

38. Stob Ghabhar East Face

For those of you who like lengthy walk-ins and steep skiing in the outback, there are some epic lines waiting for you here. Only the very occasional offpiste skier will have ventured here but there is no question that there are some high quality goods on offer. The most obvious lines drop down either side of the summit cliffs over steep but open ground. Somewhat easier skiing can also be found by dropping into the bowl from the col above Coirein Lochain. Although no descents to date are known about, perhaps even the Upper Couloir which cuts its way straight down the centre of the face from the summit may seem like a good skiing objective for the intrepid who don't mind the odd potential ice pitch.

The best route out after skiing down towards the lochan is to traverse out to skier's right aiming to get as close as possible to the col which takes you back into the Allt Toaig catchment, and from there on down to the GUM Club hut and Victoria Bridge. It would also be possible, though quite long, to ski this as part of a loop tour from the lifts. For the right party of strong skiers, a route into this remote backcountry would make for a memorable end to a North to South traverse of the Black Mount. It is also worth mentioning the potential offered by the East Face of Stob a' Choire Odhair, although a fairly lengthy walk out (probably back to Victoria Bridge along the West Highland Way) will be necessary in all but the snowiest conditions.

Loch Tulla with Clach Leathad, Meall a' Bhuiridh, and the Black Mount behind

Impressive amounts of snow in Coire na Muic

photo **Kenny Biggin** | riders **Kevin Quinn, Brian Morrison, Ed Smith**

Above the GUM Club hut

Looking across Loch Tulla en route to Stob Ghabhar

Tooling up at the snow line

Brian eyeing up future lines

photo Kenny Biggin / Ed Smith

Scoring sweet turns off Stob Ghabhar

photo **Kenny Biggin**

Stunning views towards Ben Starav

 skimountain

The Buachailles

Smack bang in the middle of Glencoe there are two long and striking ridges stretching to the South away from the road, presenting their steep and instantly recognisable northern flanks to the passing driver. These two sister mountains were named in Gaelic, generations gone by, as the Herdsmen of the Etive - one big and one small. Both mountains offer some excellent skiing opportunities and since each of them lies close to the high point of the Glencoe road they often provide the closest approach to the snowline if you're away from the lifts.

Buachaille Etive Mor

The mighty Buachaille – this spectacular mountain is an iconic sight as you drive through Glencoe, and at no time does it look better than when plastered in pristine white snow. There is a real mix of skiing on Buachaille Etive Mor, from wide open and easy bowls, right through to high end steep skiing lines, no doubt with some unskied lines waiting for the right conditions.

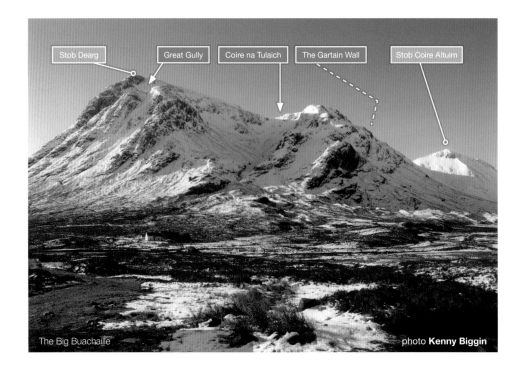

Stob Dearg Great Gully Coire na Tulaich The Gartain Wall Stob Coire Altuim

The Big Buachaille

photo **Kenny Biggin**

BUACHAILLE
ETIVE MOR

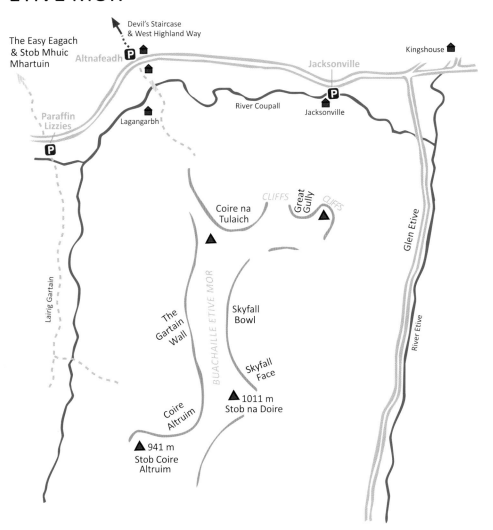

Devil's Staircase
& West Highland Way

The Easy Eagach
& Stob Mhuic
Mhartuin

Altnafeadh

Kingshouse

Jacksonville

Paraffin
Lizzies

Lagangarbh

River Coupall

Jacksonville

CLIFFS

Great
Gully

CLIFFS

Coire na
Tulaich

Glen Etive

Lairig Gartain

BUACHAILLE ETIVE MOR

The
Gartain
Wall

Skyfall
Bowl

River Etive

Skyfall
Face

Coire
Altruim

1011 m
Stob na Doire

941 m
Stob Coire
Altruim

Access

There are two main places to park for routes on the Big Buachaille – the first and highest at 320metres sits at the end of Lairig Gartain which is the glen in between Buachaille Etive Beag and Buachaille Etive Mor. There is a large layby here (Grid Ref: NN213559) and an excellent path leading off up the glen. The only slight problem is the path is on the wrong side of the River Coupall although it is usually fairly easy to cross without getting wet. The main route up from here is to continue a kilometre or so along the path, cross the burn, and then start skinning diagonally up into Coire Altruim and all the way back to the col and the ridge. From here you can do a quick jaunt up to the right onto Stob Coire Altruim, or turn left to go up onto the summits of Stob na Doire and Stob Dearg which are linked by a fine, wide ridge that is perfect for skinning along.

The alternative parking option for the Buachaille is at Altnafeadh or Lagangarbh (Grid Ref: NN221563). There is a reasonable layby on the North side of the road as well as limited parking on the rough track leading down to Lagangarbh. Parking can get pretty busy here so you may have to be inventive or even drop some people and kit off and then park the car up at the higher car park. This is the best place to park for Coire na Tulaich (described below). If you are struggling to find parking space, there is also a good sized car park down at Jacksonville (Grid Ref: NN236553, named after early doss builder Jimmy Jackson) but here you are a bit further away from most of the skiing and have to wade across the river or walk back along the road to the bridge at Lagangarbh.

39. Coire na Tulaich

similar to: Creise Bowl

More informally known as Lagangarbh corrie, the lip of this snowy bowl glints in the sunlight as you drive past and has some great skiing in it. This area has avalanched many times and there are frequently large cornices so care is required. The best place to park is at Lagangarbh from where a short walk on a good path takes you across the bridge, past Lagangarbh hut, and quickly up into a constriction that lies below the corrie. If you are skinning up it is possible to break out right fairly soon after you are above the gully – this takes you steeply onto the ridge which you can follow to the top. The ridge is steep enough that harscheissen may well be required in less than soft snow. In stable conditions without big cornices it is also possible to skin directly up into the corrie, though crampons and axe may be needed to get to the top.

There are a number of different lines that can be skied into the bowl, all of which are nice on the right day.

photo **Blair Fyffe**

Winter closing in on Lagangarbh below Coire na Tulaich

photo **Kenny Biggin** | rider **John Sutherland**

Wide enough to let rip – top third of Great Gully

Looking down the guts of Great Gully

photo **Kenny Biggin** | rider **John Sutherland**

Halfway up Great Gully – the perfect spot to try out new boots & skis

photo **Kenny Biggin** | rider **John Sutherland**

40. Great Gully

similar to:	Summit Gully
harder than:	West Gully, Central Gully (Ben Lui)

This fantastic line is one of the longest steep(ish) descents in the book and is undoubtedly one of the standout Glencoe classics. Despite the fact that climbers frequently use it for descent, and its visibility from the main road, very few ski descents of it are known about. As you look at the prominent northern face of the Big Buachaille from the A82, Great Gully is a large snowy gully some way to the left of Coire na Tulaich. The best view of the gully can be seen from around halfway along the straight that leads South-East from Lagangarbh. The base

Great Gully on the Big Buachaille beckoning to passing skiers

of the gully can either be accessed by walking over the bridge at Lagangarbh and then following the path that skirts round under the face, or by parking a little further down the road at Jacksonville and then wading across the river. The latter approach is more direct but obviously involves getting cold feet (which many skiers will need little extra help with when taking this route on).

You can ski directly into the gully almost from the summit of Stob Dearg, so you could choose to access it via Coire na Tulaich. Many will choose to climb up the gully first to ascertain conditions and scope out the logistics of the waterfall that represents the main difficulty and bars the exit of the gully. In rare conditions the waterfall collects a fair amount of snow, but as it's quite low down it seems unlikely it will ever be skiable. Most common will be for some steep scrambling to be required on the rocky buttress that lies to skier's right of the gully.

Author's Note: Ski descents of Skyfall Bowl and Great Gully amongst others feature in the SkiMountain Diaries short film episodes which you can find on the SkiMountain website. There are a number of other hard lines that have skiing potential in this area on the Buachaille but no descents are known about to date.

As with other steep gullies in the book, good snow conditions are required for successful descents of Great Gully – in lean and icy conditions there can be pitches of up to Grade III climbing standard here, so do your homework prior to committing and be prepared.

41. Skyfall Bowl

similar to:	Monument
combine with:	Gartain Wall, Coire Altruim

Many people skiing the Big Buachaille will be after a more relaxing day out than the likes of Great Gully, and Skyfall Bowl offers just that. The bowl drops down into Coire Cloiche Finne which forms a large amphitheatre up above the River Etive. There is a wide range of entrance choices here, with similar lines dropping in most of the way along the ridge, so there should be something to suit most people. Since this bowl is South facing, there is rarely enough snow to make the ski all the way down into Glen Etive good, so many will opt to ski the top part of the bowl down to a natural flattening and then skin back up onto the main ridge – from there it is easier to descend back to the car via either the Gartain Wall or Coire Altruim since these routes are more snow sure.

Author's Note: The name comes from the fact that they filmed part of the James Bond film Skyfall down below in Glen Etive. The area also has another link with 007 since the author of the Bond books Ian Fleming was part of the family who own Black Mount Estate which includes the land

photo **Kenny Biggin** | rider **John Sutherland**

Mellow turns in the sunshine in Skyfall Bowl

© SkiMountain

that the lifts are built on. The Fleming Family bought a second hand piste machine in the eighties as a present for the ski resort (it was their first piste machine). It came from the resort of Murren in Switzerland and had been used for a stunt scene in one of the early Bond films. The 'wee piste basher' as it became known later got taken out by a wet snow slide in the Canyon. There is also a memorial to Ian Fleming's brother Peter below the East Wall towards the West Highland Way. Whether the rumours that SkiMountain team skier John played the part of Daniel Craig's butt double in Skyfall are true or not, we couldn't possibly say.

42. Skyfall Face

harder than: Skyfall Bowl

Dropping down almost directly from the summit of Stob na Doire is one of those lines that to a skier just looks like it needs a set of tracks carved down it. The skiing here is a little steeper than the rest of Skyfall Bowl, though never scarily so. There can of course be large cornices on top, but apart from that... what are you waiting for?

photo Kenny Biggin | rider John Sutherland

Skyfall Face waiting for tracks

⚠ skimountain

43. The Gartain Wall

harder than: Coire Altruim

combine with: Skyfall Bowl

Crossing the Coupall in Lairig Gartain
photo **Kenny Biggin**

Towering above the River Coupall and the Lairig Gartain down below, the impressive main ridge of the Buachaille stretches between Stob na Doire and the Western top of Stob Dearg. For much of the way along this part of the ridge it is possible to ski the North West flank that drops down into Lairig Gartain. Because of the aspect, the snow here can get quite scoured, but there are a number of burn gullies that tend to hold onto the snow reasonably well. The skiing here is steep enough to require good conditions but never too worrying, and this makes a good route to use to get back reasonably close to a car parked at the upper car park.

Finding the flow on the Gartain Wall
photo **Kenny Biggin** | rider **John Sutherland**

photo **Kenny Biggin**

44. Coire Altruim

1-2

similar to: Skyfall Bowl

This corrie is largely hidden from the road and in ski boots is slightly further away from the car than many other routes. However, apart from a bit of a walk to start with, this is a great way up onto the Buachaille – in fact, this is probably the easiest route up – and is also a superb way to ski down having traversed along the main ridge from Coire na Tulaich. The easiest route down is to stay on the ridge until the col and then slide in from there. The more adventurous can ski into the corrie from higher up either on the Stob na Doire side (North West facing) or up onto the North East Face of Stob Coire Altruim which can look very impressive from the road. When skiing out it is well worth trying to ease the pain of the walk out by traversing as far as possible to skier's right before crossing the burn.

Buachaille Etive Beag

The Wee Buachaille as it's affectionately known is a long ridge, connecting three summits, that lies alongside and parallel to its big brother Buachaille Etive Mor. Of all the mountains included in this book, Buachaille Etive Beag is the one you are most likely to be able to ski from and back to the car. A good car park (Grid Ref: NN188562) sits at just under 300metres and from here you don't have far to go before you can skin diagonally up towards the ridge. The point to aim for is the main col on the ridge at Grid Ref: NN187545 – from here there are a choice of descents as described below.

45. 902 Face

similar to: East Ridge

The shortest and most accessible outing up Buachaille Etive Beag is to follow the route of the summer walking path by skinning up to the main col and then turn right to climb up onto the North East top of Stob Dubh which sits at a height of 902metres. Many will want to continue along the ridge to Stob Dubh's main summit, but for those who are ready to ski from here there is good skiing on offer down below. You can either ski off Northwards straight from the summit or the easier option is to retrace your steps back towards the col and ski down from there. The terrain is fairly open and not too steep. As you get lower there are lots of small gully lines which aren't really a problem in themselves except for the fact that they hamper you traversing back towards the car - probably the best ploy is to cross the majority of them reasonably high up.

46. Raineach Burn

similar to: 902 Face

Even closer to the road than the 902 Face, is the North Face of Stob Coire Raineach. There is an obvious gully holding a burn that cuts its way down the left of the face, and both this and the face up above it can offer good skiing. You can access this by doing a loop – starting off up the Lairig Eilde and up onto the ridge at the col, then back over the summit of Stob Coire Raineach and back down towards the car. The slope is nice and open without too much steepness to it, although in lean conditions look out for rocks.

BUACHAILLE ETIVE BEAG

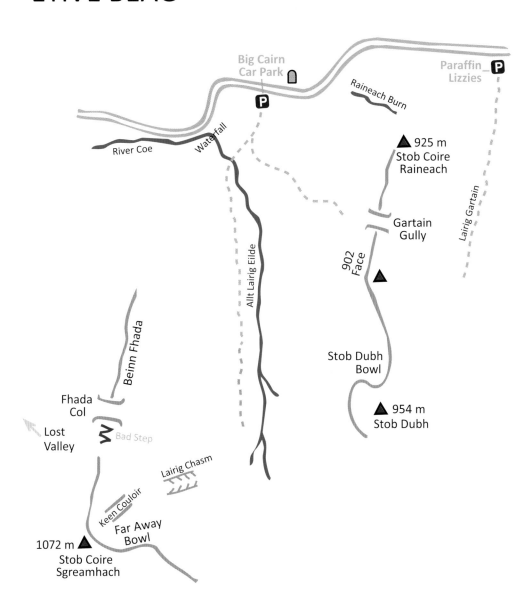

Big Cairn Car Park

Paraffin Lizzies

Raineach Burn

River Coe

Waterfall

▲ 925 m
Stob Coire Raineach

Gartain Gully

902 Face

Lairig Gartain

Allt Lairig Eilde

▲

Beinn Fhada

Stob Dubh Bowl

Fhada Col

▲ 954 m
Stob Dubh

Lost Valley

Bad Step

Lairig Chasm

Keen Couloir

Far Away Bowl

1072 m ▲
Stob Coire Sgreamhach

47. Stob Dubh Bowl

harder than: 902 Face

This is the far corrie on the Northern side of the Wee Buachaille. It tends to be the best part of the mountain at holding snow, although the summit is still not all that high at 958metres. As with the 902 Face, the choice of line is entirely open to preference and there isn't too much to watch out for other than a gully which begins two thirds of the way down the bowl. Having committed to skiing this corrie, it is probably just as well to ski all the way down the fall line to the Allt Lairig Eilde, at which point you can cross over and join the good path that lies on the far side that leads back to the car park after a kilometre or so.

The Eastern flank of the Wee Buachaille   photo **Kenny Biggin**

© SkiMountain

Buachaille Etive Beag on the right with the North East Face of Stob Coire Altruim on the left

photo **Kenny Biggin**

48. Gartain Gully

1

similar to: 902 Face

On the odd occasion when conditions dictate that skiing Southern aspects are the way forward, this route provides an excellent easy route that can also be made into a good loop that works in either direction. If you are doing the loop, park one car at the end of Lairig Gartain and another at the end of Lairig Eilde, or plan to hitch (which usually works well in Glencoe as there are plenty of like-minded folk around). This route takes you down either from the top of the 902 peak, or from the col, down in a South Easterly direction into the Lairig Gartain and the headwaters of the River Coupall. Follow the line of the broad gully and make sure you take time to spy your next outing over in Coire Altruim on the Big Buachaille. Try not to let it put you off but there's a 2km walk out from here along a good path in the Lairig Gartain.

Bidean nam Bian Massif

As you drive through Glencoe, one of the most imposing pieces of scenery is the geological architecture of the Bidean nam Bian massif. The massif consists of four main mountains linked together by a series of ridges. The ridges of Beinn Fhada, Gearr Aonach, and Aonach Dubh extend out towards the road and their rocky buttresses are collectively known as The Three Sisters. The Western-most sister, Aonach Dubh, has the gaping chasm of Ossian's Cave adorning its crags, which legend has it was the birthplace of the eponymous bard. The main mountains making up the massif are Stob Coire nan Lochan, Stob Coire nam Beith, Stob Coire Sgreamhach, and Bidean nam Bian itself. In amongst this complex and iconic clump of mountains are some of the most rewarding offpiste ski routes in the area.

Car Parks in The Coe

If you are new to Glencoe, it can take a while to get to grips with where everything is. The various mountains rise up steeply either side of the road, and knowing where to stop and park for the different hills plays a large part in starting to feel at home here. Over the years the locals and in particular the mountain rescue team members have built up a rich selection of names for the various laybys and car parks, and knowing where these all are is a great way to get your bearings.

The pristine slopes of Bidean above the Lost Valley

GLENCOE CAR PARKS

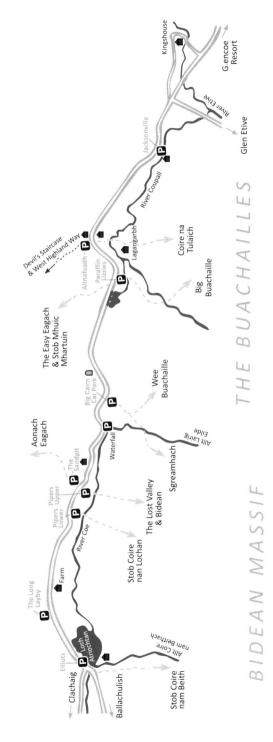

AONACH EAGACH

THE BUACHAILLES

BIDEAN MASSIF

Kingshouse

Glencoe Resort

River Etive

Glen Etive

Jacksonville

River Coupall

Devil's Staircase & West Highland Way

Altnafeadh

Paraffin Lizzies

Lagangarbh

Coire na Tulaich

Big Buachaille

The Easy Eagach & Stob Mhuic Mhartuin

Big Cairn Car Park

Wee Buachaille

Aonach Eagach

Allt Lairig Eilde

The Sandpit

Waterfall

Sgreamhach

Pipers Upper

Pipers Lower

The Lost Valley & Bidean

River Coe

Stob Coire nan Lochan

The Long Layby

Farm

Loch Atriochtan

Allt Coire nam Beithach

Elliots

Clachaig

Ballachulish

Stob Coire nam Beith

skimountain

The following labels appear on the photograph:

Bidean nam Bian | Stob Coire nan Lochan | Stob Coire nam Beith

Stob Coire Sgreamhach | Lost Valley | Broad Gully

Ossians

The Bidean Massif from Aonach Eagach

photo **Kenny Biggin**

Coire nan Lochan

Stob Coire nan Lochan is the most accessible area of the Bidean nam Bian massif and as such is very popular with winter climbers and winter skills groups. The large corrie which holds the lochans faces generally North East and therefore also does a great job of catching and holding snow. In fact, this corrie will often be the snowiest in the glen since it has the entire Bidean massif acting as a snow-catcher for it. Although there's a strenuous walk in up to the snow-line, once you put your head down it doesn't take too long, and while up there it is (fitness permitting) fairly easy to do several laps. As with the Lost Valley, the lochans also make a fine winter camping spot.

Access

Driving from the North, after passing Loch Achtriochtan the road starts to climb – the parking for Stob Coire nan Lochan is the first large layby on the South side of the road known as Pipers Lower. From the car park walk directly down the bank to the river where a path leads you across the River Coe. Follow the path steeply up towards the snow. Around two thirds of the way up there is a short, tricky rocky section on the path which when icy requires care, but beyond that you quickly come into the main corrie and often you can put your skins on here. Once out of the gorge you have a choice of which way to go – the easiest option being to cross the burn and branch out to your right, over a couple of steepenings and then up onto Stob Coire nan Lochan's North Ridge which rises up from Aonach Dubh. Following this route takes you fairly gently up the ridge towards Broad Gully and will be the route of choice for most.

Slightly more adventurous is heading out to the left up onto the North East Ridge coming from Gearr Aonach. It is easy to get onto the ridge but there are a couple of rocky steps on the way to the summit which are likely to require a little scrambling and perhaps crampons. Of course climbing directly up one of the gullies is an option too but beware of dangers from above if you choose that approach.

Perfect skinning terrain in Coire nan Lochan

Still smiling before the walk in at the bottom of the Coire nan Lochan path

photo **Kenny Biggin** | riders **Ian Lloyd, Alan Muir, Scott Aston**

STOB COIRE
nan LOCHAN

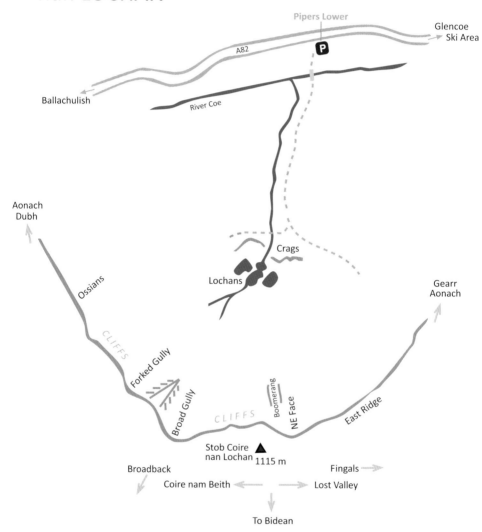

Pipers Lower

Glencoe
Ski Area

A82

Ballachulish

River Coe

Aonach
Dubh

Ossians

Crags

Lochans

Gearr
Aonach

CLIFFS

Forked Gully

Broad Gully

CLIFFS

Boomerang

NE Face

East Ridge

Stob Coire
nan Lochan 1115 m

Broadback

Fingals →

Coire nam Beith ← → Lost Valley

To Bidean

© SkiMountain

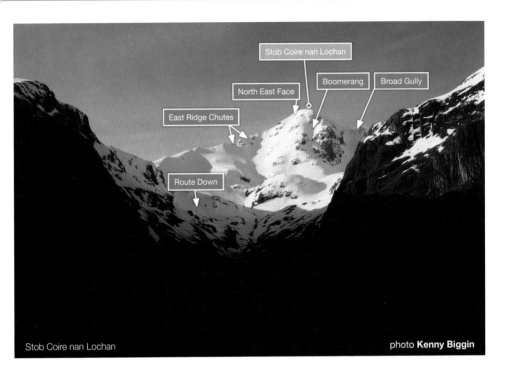

Stob Coire nan Lochan

photo **Kenny Biggin**

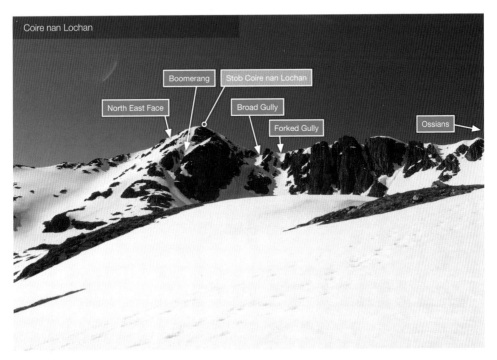

Coire nan Lochan

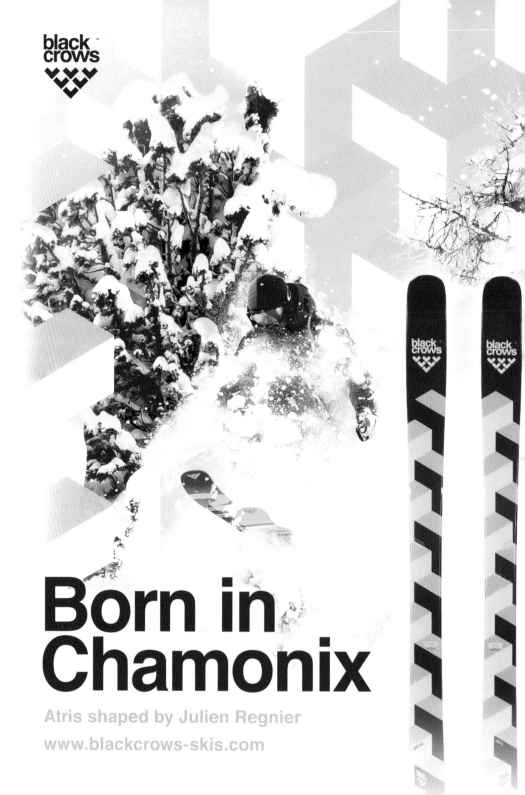

49. Ossians

1-3

similar to:	The East Ridge
combine with:	Broad Gully

In a snowy winter, the trudge up the path into the corrie reveals some fantastic freeride terrain. One of the most accessible parts of the corrie to ski lies over on the right as you look up – this area lies above the col on the North Ridge that leads to Aonach Dubh. This is also the easiest way off from the summit of Stob Coire nan Lochan and the route to aim for if the mist rolls in when on the top. In between the cliffs and the col there are a number of nice open and not too steep lines dropping down off the ridge. Closer to the cliffs things steepen up and you can pick your way through the rock bands in several places. The choice of route is yours and the lines here are somewhat short. You will reach the lochan all too quickly but a short skin will take you back up to the ridge so why not do multiple laps? It is possible to ski down either side of the corrie from the lochan so long as you avoid the small crags that lie in the middle of the basin underneath the lochan.

The name for this part of the corrie comes from the fact that the large gash in the cliffs on the road side of Aonach Dubh is known as Ossian's Cave. Although in 1762 James MacPherson managed to translate and retell many of Ossian's epic 3rd Century poems, he missed out anything about the ancient bard being the first to have a wee shot at skiing on the slopes of Stob Coire nan Lochan, back in the day. See also the route description for Fingals as that route is the big daddy of Ossians and drops to the South East from the top of Stob Coire nan Lochan into the Lost Valley.

photo **Kenny Biggin** | rider **Scott Aston**

Ossian's freeride area in Coire nan Lochan

50. Traverse of Stob Coire nan Lochan

A great way to explore Stob Coire nan Lochan is to do a traverse - up the East Ridge, over the summit, and down the North Ridge. Walk up in to Coire nan Lochan in the normal way and as soon as the snow allows, start heading out to your left making for the ridge. The route up the East Ridge takes you over a couple of tricky rock steps that will require some easy scrambling and may well need axe and crampons. Once on the summit you can take your time gazing across to Bidean nam Bian before heading off down the North Ridge. A short descent takes you to the obvious large entrance at the top of Broad Gully, then past the more fierce entrance of Forked Gully. Keep back from the edge as there are often large cornices along this ridge until you get past the main cliffs and can drop down off the ridge into the corrie at Ossians. A harder variation of this traverse would be to come up onto Gearr Aonach and the East Ridge via the Zig Zags climbing route.

51. Broad Gully

similar to: Monument, Baillies

As the name suggests this is a nice wide open gully and a route that in the right conditions is accessible to a wide range of skiers. You get a great view of Broad Gully from the car park, and as such this is a good line to go and do so that you can look up into the corrie in years to come knowing that you've 'been there, done that'. One of the problems with Broad Gully is that it gets used extensively by winter climbers – both to access the bottom of routes but also as a descent – so the snow is frequently littered with footprints. You also need to be careful when skiing it that you aren't knocking sluff etc. down onto unsuspecting climbers. The entrance to the gully is very obvious from the ridge and there aren't usually too many difficulties getting into the top of it. There is a slight narrowing and steepening halfway down which can create a bit of a bulge and a convexity, but the gully still remains nice and wide and rarely all that difficult here.

Looking up Broad Gully - Soft in the sun, ice in the shade

photo **Kenny Biggin** | riders **Katie & Neil Fleming**

Nice snow in Broad Gully

photo **Kenny Biggin** | rider Jordan Tiernan

52. Forked Gully

harder than: North East Face

Forked Gully lies to skier's left of Broad Gully, the other side of a short rocky ridge climb called Dorsal Arête. This is a much steeper undertaking than Broad Gully and despite the proximity of the two gullies there is a dramatic difference in gradient between the two. Although it is called Forked Gully, from a skiing perspective only the skier's right side of the gully is an option. The entrance, scarp wall, and first few turns can feel fairly steep and exposed until you are past a narrowing about halfway down, at which point the gully starts to open out and mellow. The gully sees reasonably regular ski descents these days but was also skied by Wul Thompson back in the eighties, when he took advantage of the presence of a helicopter during the filming of a Blue Peter episode featuring Caron Keating.

At the top of Forked Gully

photo **Jordan Tiernan** | rider **Kenny Biggin**

Author's Note: The day I met Katie and Neil Fleming in this neck of the woods, I saw them drop into Broad Gully and could hear the echoes from the ice they hit halfway down. They climbed back up and dropped into Forked Gully despite the ice – good effort! Meanwhile, we had skied some much nicer snow on the NE Face that day so we took great pleasure in backing Katie up about the fact that really she should pick their lines in the future. Katie also took this opportunity to tell me, to my dismay, that the un-named heli-skier on the far right of a picture near the back of the Nevis guidebook, is her Mum, Lorna Stoddart... sorry I missed you out Lorna!

53. Boomerang Gully

harder than: Forked Gully

Boomerang is another line that can easily be spied from the road and makes a good tick in any skier's season. As its name suggests, the line takes a long curve through the East side of Stob Coire nan Lochan's summit cliffs. Where the gully's main bend is, there is a steep pitch which very often is either rock or ice, and this section is only sometimes skiable, so careful inspection from below or by climbing up it is advised. Some may choose to do a short rap to get over the steep pitch but note

An icy bootpack up Boomerang

photo **Kenny Biggin** | rider **Neil Muir**

Getting steeper at the entrance to Boomerang

photo **Doug Bryce** | rider **Al Reid**

that anchors can be tricky to set up here. To find the entrance to the gully from the top, start at the summit of Stob Coire nan Lochan and drop several turns down the North East Face before trending to skier's left. The gully is initially fairly open but will quickly lure you in and gets quite steep for a while until it bends back round to the left and opens out into the main bowl. Be warned that this gully gets little in the way of sunshine, so even when most of the rest of the corrie is soft, ice can remain lurking here ready to give the unwary more than they bargained for.

Finding perfection on the North East Face

54. North East Face

harder than: Broad Gully, Paradise

In a snowy year the North East Face of Stob Coire nan Lochan is a spectacular sight, clearly visible from the road, and is another great Glencoe route that allows you to ski directly from the summit. This route offers a welcome alternative to skiing in gullies and in good conditions provides a really rewarding ski. For those who feel the top pitch is too much, it is possible to make your way down the East Ridge a little until you feel happier sliding onto the face. Once off the summit, route finding is fairly straightforward and the fall line leads you naturally down into the bowl and on towards the lochans.

photo **Neil Muir** | rider **Kenny Biggin**

Getting in the flow on a North East Face variation

55. East Ridge Chutes

On the way up the East Ridge towards the summit of Stob Coire nan Lochan, there are a couple of short but nice lines dropping off the ridge to the North. These are probably not great objectives in their own right, but if the weather is closing in on your way up, or if you are doing multiple laps, these can add a welcome bit of variety.

Route Out from Coire nan Lochan

It is possible to ski either side of the rognon (the rocky outcrop) which lies below the lochans, however probably the best skiing and often the way to get lowest with your skis on is to traverse across to the Eastern bank (skier's right) of the corrie above lochan height. Stay high on this bank following several nice pitches of snow until it runs out. There may be a little scramble to get back down onto the path. On the way back down take care on the rocky step in the path and try not to get too disheartened when your complaining knees reach the bridge back across the river only to realise there is a last sting in the tail waiting for you with the walk back up to the carpark. What makes this last climb back up to the road worse is the fact you are often being watched by a busload of tourists so not only do you have to keep going at a good pace all the way up, but also maintain the illusion of finding it easy – good luck.

Other Aspects

Although the bulk of the skiing on Stob Coire nan Lochan is in the main corrie, there are also some fine lines dropping off the back and side of the mountain. There are two main routes – one heading into the Lost Valley, the other heading into Coire nam Beith. It is also well worth traversing across to Bidean nam Bian via the South Ridge from the summit, and along the way you have the option of either dropping into the Lost Bowl to skier's left, or Diamond Col to skier's right (see descriptions later on).

56. Fingals

| harder than: | Ossians, Lost Bowl |
| combine with: | Traverse of Stob Coire nan Lochan |

Not to be outdone by his son Ossian, Highland skiing folklore has it that Fingal's favourite route was to ski from the top of Stob Coire nan Lochan down its South East flank all the way down into the Lost Valley. When it has snow this is a fine route that lies to skier's left of the Lost Bowl (see Bidean – Lost Valley section). Although it doesn't hold snow as long as North facing alternatives, if you catch it at the right time it drops all the way from the summit down a continuous pitch of almost 600metres.

As the name suggests, this route is the big daddy of Ossians in Coire nan Lochan. Legend tells that Fingal was a 3rd century Scottish king, popularised in modern literature by James MacPherson's translations of Ossian's epic poems. Whether these characters were in fact Scottish or Irish, whether they ever existed, and whether the Ossian cycle of verse was in fact written by Ossian is all up for debate, however there can be little doubt that if Ossian and Fingal did exist, they must have loved the freeride potential that Glencoe has to offer.

Skinning up Stob Coire nan Lochan's North Ridge

57. Broadback

The West face of Stob Coire nan Lochan drops fairly uniformly down into Coire nam Beith. The terrain here is littered with loose boulders and scree but there are often continuous lines of snow leading down into the corrie. The most consistent line is from the ridge at the top of Broad Gully. Note that the section of the face directly beneath the summit is generally steep and rocky and won't usually offer nice skiing.

The route down skier's right of the corrie

photo **Kenny Biggin** | rider **Ron Cameron**

The way down after a good session in Coire nan Lochan

photo **Kenny Biggin** | riders **Katie & Neil Fleming**

Stob Coire nam Beith

As you are driving South from Glencoe village, Stob Coire nam Beith rises solidly up in front of you marking the start of the real mountains of the pass. This peak lies just North West of Bidean nam Bian and although far less well known by name, it is just as impressive to look at and from a skier's perspective offers great potential. Because the car park lies below the point where the road begins to climb, there is a more strenuous walk in to Stob Coire nam Beith (pronounced 'Stob-curah-nam-Bay') than to Bidean or Lochan, which is probably why it sees less traffic. However, the climb is only a little extra and it's well worth the effort.

It is worth noting that the car park at the end of Loch Achtriochtan is one of many places in The Coe that the micro climate can be quite misleading – it can be very windy in the car park due to the funnelling effect of the glen, but comparatively still up high (of course that pattern can be reversed as well).

photo **Kenny Biggin**

Inspiring lines on Stob Coire nam Beith   photo **Kenny Biggin**

Access

The best way into this corrie is to park at the West end of Loch Achtriochtan close to the turn off to the Clachaig. There is a picturesque white house here known locally as Elliots after its occupants. Although it may look inviting, the path doesn't go up to the house but instead starts at a gate on the far side of the road bridge across the River Coe. The path is excellent and must have been hard work to build – follow this up towards the waterfalls, over a tricky but short rocky section, until you get to the gorge. Here the right bank gets quite steep and it is generally easier to cross over the burn until it opens back out. After a while you come over a rise and into the main corrie – from here you can see up in to Church Door Buttress and Bidean on your left, with Summit Gully straight in front of you.

The easiest way to the top of Stob Coire nam Beith is to continue up the bowl straight ahead to the col at Grid Ref: NN136546. From here the ridge leads up Eastwards to the summit cairn at 1107metres.

If you decide to head up towards Bidean via the Diamond Col instead, you can break out of the main gorge early and cut upwards towards the corrie beneath some crags. A path of sorts leads up into the corrie, passing through a gate on the way (make sure you close it behind you!)

 skimountain

STOB COIRE
nam BEITH

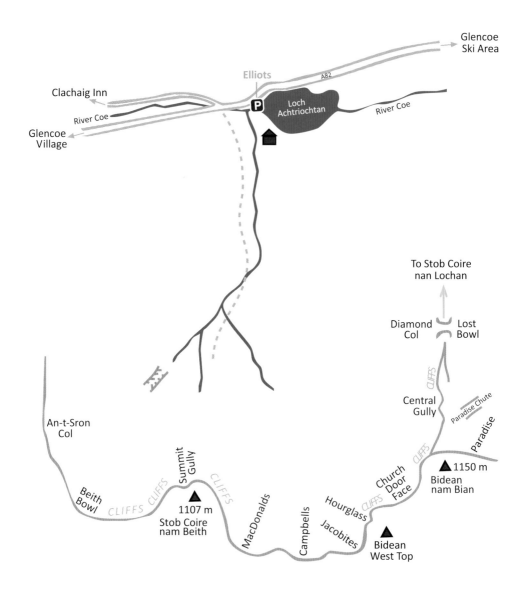

An-t-Sron
Col

Beith
Bowl

CLIFFS

CLIFFS

Summit
Gully

CLIFFS

▲ 1107 m
Stob Coire
nam Beith

MacDonalds

Campbells

Jacobites

Hourglass

CLIFFS

Church
Door
Face

▲
Bidean
West Top

Central
Gully

CLIFFS

Paradise Chute

Paradise

▲ 1150 m
Bidean
nam Bian

Diamond
Col

Lost
Bowl

To Stob Coire
nan Lochan

CLIFFS

Clachaig Inn

River Coe

Glencoe
Village

Elliots

A82

Loch
Achtriochtan

River Coe

Glencoe
Ski Area

58. Summit Gully

similar to: Great Gully

Summit Gully on Stob Coire nam Beith has to be one of the standout classic steep lines in Glencoe. You can ski into it right from the summit of the mountain and you are within the main gully for 400metres with plenty more below that. This is a feisty line and not one to be underestimated. How easy or otherwise the descent is will depend hugely on conditions, so scoping it out well from below (or climbing up it first) is very important. The route in from the summit drops in about five metres to skier's left of the cairn, so you can't really miss it. Once in the gully there are a number of route finding decisions to be made since there are some large rock islands and other features splitting the gully into various strands. Which variation is most skiable on a particular day will depend on how the snow has blown in, although sticking to skier's right worked well for the author.

There are often short rock or icy pitches to negotiate but thankfully with enough snow the whole line fills up nicely.

Author's Note: There may be more steep skiing potential to be explored on this North Face, although

The obligatory selfie, taken dropping into Summit Gully

photo **Kenny Biggin**

it is a serious place with complex route finding and a rope is almost certain to be needed elsewhere on this face. When on the summit of Stob Coire nam Beith make sure you take the chance to scope out the steep lines which drop from Bidean – this is probably the best vantage point, especially for Hourglass.

59. Beith Bowl

| similar to: | Dragon Bowl |

Often the normal hillwalker's route up a mountain offers the easiest ski route, and this is certainly true in this case. Beith Bowl lies to skier's left of the big cliffs of Stob Coire nam Beith's North Face. There is some fantastic skiing here and it is usually possible to pick an entry to avoid cornices. If you are skiing down to this bowl off the summit, perhaps after traversing across from Bidean, note that the ridge itself can be scoured and you may want to use crampons and axe to get down to the start of the bowl. Dropping in higher up the ridge provides steeper lines, while going from the col is usually fairly easy. The bowl flattens out very quickly which makes this a good place for practising skills and doing multiple laps. Be wary though of the large gorge terrain trap that lies towards the base of the bowl.

Easy skiing in the Beith Bowl

photo **Kenny Biggin**

© SkiMountain

60. An-t-Sron Col

similar to: Beith Bowl

The long ridge that stretches North away from Stob Coire nam Beith is called An-t-Sron and is the unfortunate fourth sister not to be counted when the Three Sisters were named. Although it perhaps lacks the grandeur of the likes of Aonach Dubh, Gearr Aonach, and Beinn Fhada, there is still some cracking skiing to be had here. There is an obvious col on the ridge at roughly Grid Ref: NN135550 and below this there is a pleasant mini-bowl that makes an alternative route up or a good option for a second run if you've already skied the main Beith Bowl.

61. Number 2 Gully

Above the car park at Elliots there are a number of serious and low lying gullies where some skiing may be possible given enough snow, but while these might be nice to look at, the real classics lie higher up. The only gully in this lower section of the mountain known to have seen a descent (by Martin Burrows-Smith back in the early '80s) is Number 2 Gully which is the largest and most obvious. Climbing it first is recommended, but if approaching from the top it can be found from the ridge leading to Aonach Dubh from Stob Coire nan Lochan. The bottom half of the gully will almost certainly be unskiable, although escaping onto the bottom of Dinner Time Buttress may be possible. Caution is advised!

Stob Coire nam Beith on the right and the West Face of Stob Coire nan Lochan. Note Number 2 Gully to the right of the telegraph pole

photo **Kenny Biggin**

62. Massacre Face

similar to: Local Hero, Ghlais Face

As you ski off the summit of Stob Coire nam Beith towards the West Top of Bidean, you quickly come to an open snow face to the skier's right of some cliffs. This face is split into two by a large rocky rib. South of the rib is called Campbells, while North (skier's left) of the rib is named MacDonalds. There is a real big mountain feel to these lines and although neither are particularly steep, a ski all the way down into the corrie feels well worth the effort of getting up there in the first place. MacDonalds will normally require a traverse out to skier's right to avoid the rock bands lower down.

The naming comes from the Massacre of Glencoe of 1692 where almost 40 Jacobite sympathetic MacDonalds were killed by their 'guests' the Campbells. Around forty more women and children died of exposure afterwards since their houses were burnt down. Be careful who you invite round to stay!

photo **Dave Biggin** | rider **Kenny Biggin**

Climbing back up Campbells for that crucial second run

Bidean nam Bian

Bidean nam Bian is the highest mountain in the Glencoe area, and at 1150metres with a shapely summit this is the peak that stands out in views from afar. As befitting the highest peak in the area, it also boasts some (not all) of the hardest skiing. But all is not lost for the more discerning offpiste skier as there are a myriad of more friendly lines dropping from Bidean's dizzying heights.

Bidean nam Bian – Beith Side

There are two very distinct sides to the skiing on Bidean – to the West is Coire nam Beith with famous lines such as Central Gully and Hourglass, while to the East is Coire Gabhail or the Lost Valley. It is quite possible to ski one of these areas and be oblivious to the terrain on offer on the other side, but be inquisitive and take a look because the skiing on offer here is right up there with the best. The Coire nam Beith side of Bidean is demarcated by a series of well known climbing crags, with Diamond and Church Door buttresses adorning the North Western flank of Bidean's main summit. While the West Top of Bidean, a subsidiary summit, lies a few hundred metres to the West and plays host to Bishop's Buttress and Hourglass Gully. The routes to skier's left of Bidean's West Top actually join with the Massacre Face of Stob Coire nam Beith so these sections should be read together.

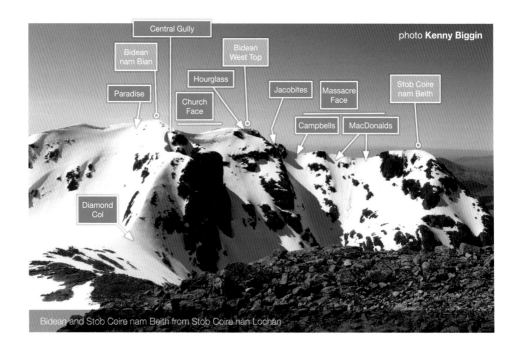

photo **Kenny Biggin**

Bidean and Stob Coire nam Beith from Stob Coire nan Lochan

© SkiMountain

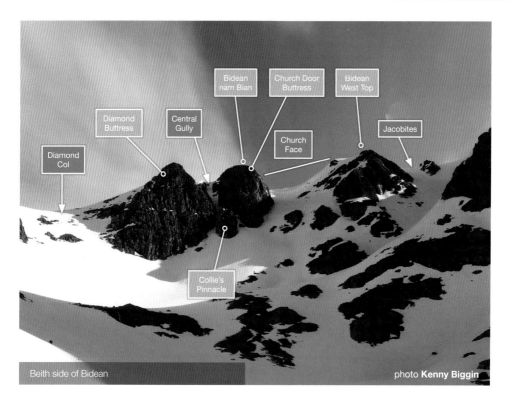

Diamond Col

Diamond Buttress

Central Gully

Bidean nam Bian

Church Door Buttress

Bidean West Top

Church Face

Jacobites

Collie's Pinnacle

Beith side of Bidean

photo **Kenny Biggin**

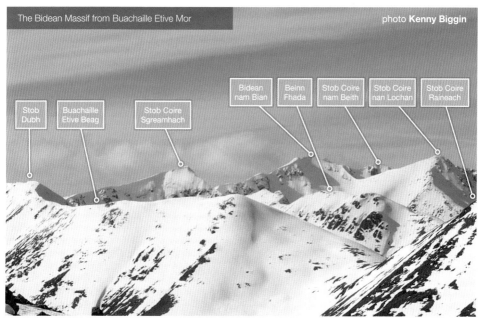

The Bidean Massif from Buachaille Etive Mor

photo **Kenny Biggin**

Stob Dubh

Buachaille Etive Beag

Stob Coire Sgreamhach

Bidean nam Bian

Beinn Fhada

Stob Coire nam Beith

Stob Coire nan Lochan

Stob Coire Raineach

Always a relief to get past the hard bit – the bottom of Hourglass

63. Jacobites

harder than: Massacre Face

For those who take a look down Hourglass and decide (sensibly some might say) that it's not for them, there is a consolation prize in this wider, shorter, and less steep alternative. The entrance lies just below and to the left of the cliffs of Bidean's West Top. Although substantially easier than Hourglass, there is still plenty to think about for the top few turns until it opens out and joins with Campbells below a rocky island.

64. Hourglass Gully

harder than: Jacobites

This is one of the harder lines on Bidean that doesn't often see ski descents. Hourglass lives up to its name with a nice wide entrance to lure you in at the top, followed by a distinct narrowing, before it widens out at the bottom. You can find the top of the gully with ease as it is ten metres or so to skier's right of the cairn on the West Top of Bidean. The narrow section is the crux and although the gully is steep, it is the combination of the lack of width plus the angle that makes it tricky. As anyone who has done it will tell you, it looks steeper than it actually is from over on Stob Coire nam Beith… but then they would say that, wouldn't they? Make sure to check the line carefully before dropping in as it often has breaks or icy steps in it.

Kenny taking his time in Hourglass

photo **Dave Biggin** | rider **Kenny Biggin**

Hourglass on the right, Diamond Col on the left... taken from Stob Coire nam Beith

photo **Kenny Biggin**

© SkiMountain

65. The Church Face

similar to: Jacobites

For those of you who don't fancy the look of either Central or Hourglass, this line is a fair bit more open but still drops steeply down between the high crags. This face lies in between Bidean's main summit and the West Top and there are a variety of lines to choose from here, some more exposed and exciting than others. It should be noted that this face is well known for avalanching most seasons and there have been serious incidents here. The easiest line sticks in the middle of the bowl, roughly halfway between the two summits, however with good snow (and the right mentality) there are also possibilities for dropping directly off either summit. After passing through the crags the slope opens out into the wide open corrie below making this a great route to do top to bottom.

66. Central Gully

harder than: Church Face

combine with: Hourglass

A real tick by any gully-bagger's standards, Central Gully is one of those lines that memories are made of. When in the gully you are deep in between the massive rock walls of Diamond Buttress (on skier's right) and Church Door Buttress (on skier's left). Looking down the gully from the top the view to the bottom is obscured by Collie's Pinnacle, another well known feature for climbers. The bottom of Central Gully splits in two around Collie's Pinnacle – skier's right branch is narrower and a little steeper, while skier's left starts off fairly open but ends up in a narrowing. Both branches can have short rock or ice pitches. Most will choose skier's left, but be prepared to take a bit of air to get you over the pitch (or set up a short rappel), and provided the snow conditions are forgiving enough the corrie then opens out giving you plenty of time and space to regain control and bleed off your speed.

To get into the gully in the first place, you need to descend the ridge from the top of Bidean towards Stob Coire nan Lochan for around 100metres. There are actually two entry options at the top, although the skier's left will usually be most appealing. Most seasons will see Central Gully release slides; indeed the earliest avalanche incident attended here by Glencoe Mountain Rescue was on the 5th November (Bonfire Night).

Author's Note: The unusual depth of snow in the winter of 2014 was enough to bank out the pitch to skier's left of the pinnacle, but by the time we got round to skiing it a large slot had opened up - as seen in the Central Gully episode of the SkiMountain Diaries which you can find and watch on the SkiMountain website.

Enjoying last turns of the season in Central Gully

Dave checking Central Gully 'goes'...

67. Diamond Col

	similar to:	Ossians
1		
	combine with:	Lost Bowl

Sitting halfway in between Stob Coire nan Lochan and Bidean nam Bian, there's a large col in a spectacular setting that provides fantastic easy skiing opportunities to either side. The route described here drops down to the North West with Diamond Buttress on skier's left, however it is equally possible (though a little steeper) to ski off the other side into the Lost Bowl to the South East. There are usually numerous patches of rocks peeping above the snow here, but in most winters it is easy to find a wide and forgiving line to ski down into the corrie. This is a great line to take either to link a traverse from the Lost Valley over into Coire nam Beith, or if the steep ridge leading up above to Bidean has put you off and you need an easy escape route.

Great easy skiing on Diamond Col

Diamond Col, Central Gully, and Church Face

photo **Kenny Biggin**

ROSSIGNOL
another best day

Bidean nam Bian – Lost Side

If you have never walked into Coire Gabhail it is well worth an outing with or without skis as it holds a fantastic remnant from Scotland's glacial past, the Lost Valley. This feature lies in between the Eastern most of the Three Sisters, Gearr Aonach and Beinn Fhada. From the road there is little to distinguish the glen from its neighbour Coire nan Lochan, but once you climb up to around 300metres the glen dramatically opens out into a large flat plain that it is easy to imagine being full of the MacDonalds' cattle. Beyond the Lost Valley, there is a huge and complex headwall with Bidean nam Bian at its Western end and Stob Coire Sgreamhach to the East. The summit of Stob Coire nan Lochan also lies up above. After a good snowfall, there is a multitude of great terrain here, and as a place to ski in Scotland this is surely a 'must visit' destination.

Access

The best place to park for the Lost Valley is at Upper Pipers. From here a path leads out of the East end of the car park down to a track (part of the old road). Follow this East for a couple of hundred metres to where the path leads down to the river. There is a long metal staircase leading down to the bridge over the River Coe with a good path on the far side. Follow the path up, through a gate, and continue up until the gorge starts to close in. There is an art to recognising the right point at which to cross over the burn to walk up the left bank. If you find yourself scrabbling around amongst boulders and trees, retrace your steps and cross over the burn as the path is significantly better here. Follow

Bidean from Stob Coire Sgreamhach

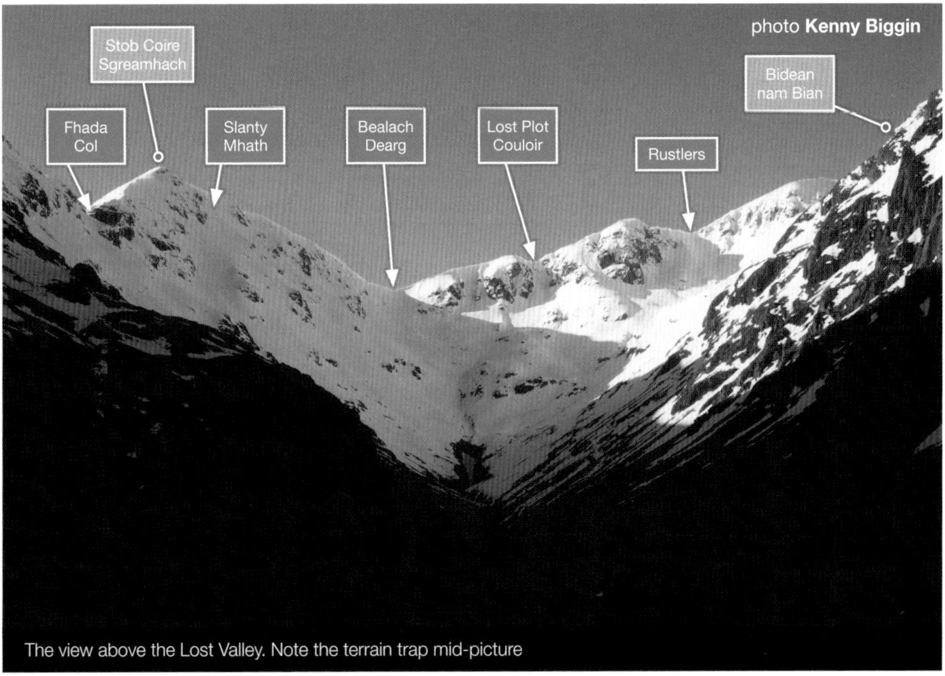
photo Kenny Biggin
Stob Coire Sgreamhach
Bidean nam Bian
Fhada Col
Slanty Mhath
Bealach Dearg
Lost Plot Couloir
Rustlers
The view above the Lost Valley. Note the terrain trap mid-picture

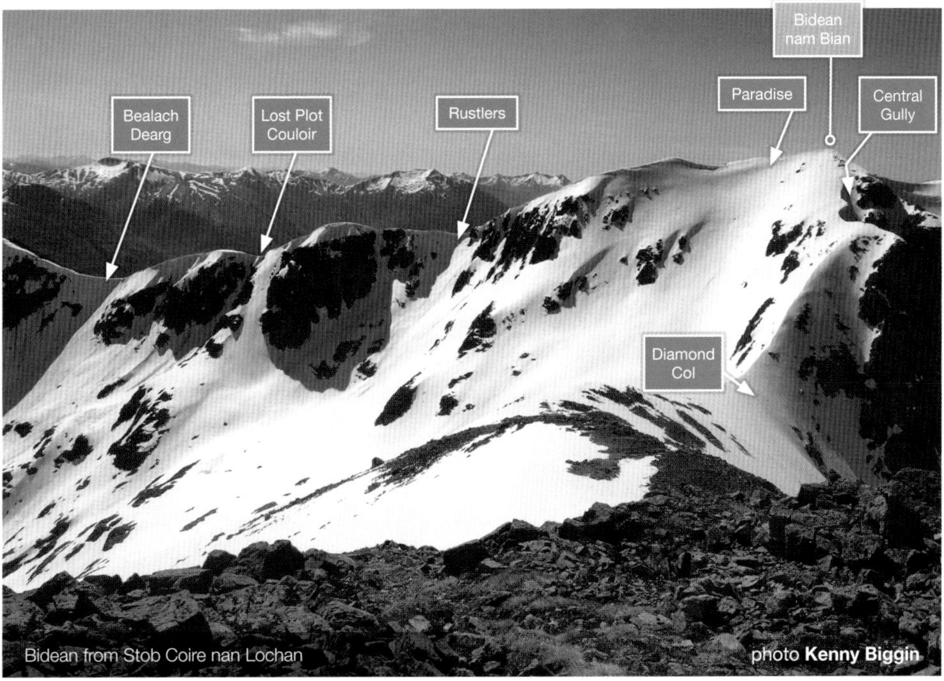
Bidean nam Bian
Paradise
Central Gully
Bealach Dearg
Lost Plot Couloir
Rustlers
Diamond Col
photo Kenny Biggin
Bidean from Stob Coire nan Lochan

Bootpacking up the ridge from Stob Coire nan Lochan to Bidean

The classic first view of the Lost Valley

this path which takes you high up on the Eastern bank of the burn to a point where the view of the glen opens up in front of you and reminds you that this would be an excellent place to stop for a rest and a sarnie.

After crossing the Lost Valley, follow the route of the path on the Northern bank of the chasm which leads up into the corrie. Although this part is usually quite innocuous, be careful in avalanche or icy conditions here, as this would be a horrible place to take a fall. Towards the end of the chasm you can choose whether to continue directly ahead to go up the main col in-between Bidean and Sgreamhach, or alternatively branch up to your right and aim for the col in between Bidean and Stob Coire nan Lochan. Either way, the skinning is straightforward at first, but steepens up at the end so be prepared to use harscheissen, axe, or crampons as required.

If your aim is to go to the summit of Bidean, the ridge leading from Stob Coire Sgreamhach is more gentle than the ridge leading from Stob Coire nan Lochan which has a short but steep snow slope that non-mountaineers may find quite exposed, although it doesn't require any actual climbing. In some ways the easiest route up onto Bidean is actually to go up Stob Coire nam Beith first, and then follow the ridge round via the West Top – the climb up to the col on that route is slightly easier than that encountered when approaching from the Lost Valley side.

Route Out of the Lost Valley

The way down is fairly obvious, but it makes a big difference to make sure you pick up the path out of the Lost Valley at the right spot. About three quarters of the way across the plain, the path starts on the right hand side and stays well up high above the bouldery complications at the mouth of the glen. It is always easier to find this path once you have come up it once via the right route. On your way back to the car after a long day it is always a welcome sight to see the bridge back across the Coe, the only thing being that you must now go uphill one last time to get back up to your car.

68. The Lost Bowl

combine with: Diamond Col

From Diamond Col that lies in between Stob Coire nan Lochan and Bidean, there is a large open bowl with some of the best easy skiing on the Bidean massif. You can drop in from pretty much anywhere along the ridge and get a nice long ski down into the corrie. Since this is a concave bowl, skiing here should be a little less consequential than elsewhere and provides a nice introduction to the area without having to take on anything more serious. It is well worth considering linking a ski here with a trip either up or down Diamond Col on the Coire nam Beith side, perhaps by skinning up The Lost Bowl and then down Diamond Col or vice versa. Remember that these two sides of the ridge are on completely different aspects so snow conditions will vary dramatically.

THE LOST VALLEY

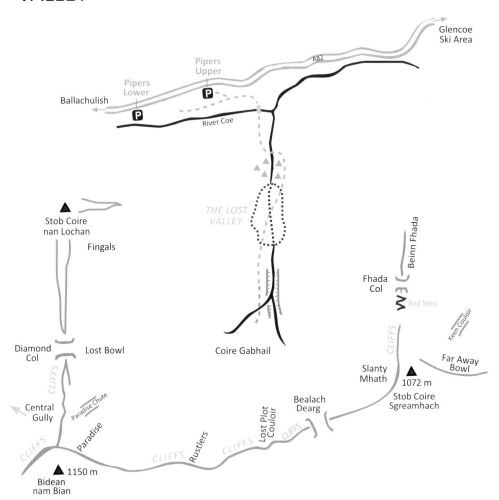

Glencoe
Ski Area

A82

Pipers
Upper

Pipers
Lower

Ballachulish

River Coe

THE LOST
VALLEY

Stob Coire
nan Lochan

Fingals

Beinn Fhada

Fhada
Col

Bad Step

Diamond
Col

Lost Bowl

Coire Gabhail

CLIFFS

Keen Couloir

Far Away
Bowl

Slanty
Mhath

1072 m

CLIFFS

Central
Gully

Paradise Chute

Paradise

Bealach
Dearg

Stob Coire
Sgreamhach

CLIFFS

CLIFFS

Rustlers

CLIFFS

Lost Plot
Couloir

CLIFFS

1150 m
Bidean
nam Bian

Looking from Bidean to the Black Mount and beyond

photo Kenny Biggin

69. Paradise

2

harder than: Lost Bowl

If you are going to ski one route in Glencoe, this would be a great choice. Conditions permitting, the line is suitable for most skiers and cuts magnificently down the North East Face, right from the summit of the highest mountain in the area. The entrance is usually straightforward since from the cairn on top of Bidean you can start with a couple of easy turns on the ridge leading towards Stob Coire nan Lochan. For the more adventurous, dropping in further to skier's right is also an option though there is often a cornice here. There is ample room to open up and get some great turns as the corrie drops several hundred metres in front of you. The gradient eases out nicely after a while and there is a good place to regroup and take pictures of your buddies on a flattening.

A little to skier's left of the main line there is also the Paradise Chute which is a nice alternative dropping down through a small rocky gully.

70. Rustlers

harder than: Church Face

Before they met their untimely end, the MacDonalds of Glencoe used the Lost Valley as a hiding place for their cattle. Whether they were hiding them from rustlers from other clans, or if they were hiding them from the people they had stolen them from themselves is unclear. Either way, surely the concept of people skiing down this dubious line at the head of the corrie would have left them bemused, though no doubt entertained also.

This line sits just above the second minor top on the ridge leading up to Bidean from the col. It is frequently corniced, and drops steeply to skier's left of Lost Valley Major Buttress. The route opens out reasonably quickly, but getting in at the top and the first few turns are likely to be pretty full on.

Looking up Paradise to Bidean, with entrances to Central Gully and Diamond Col off the ridge to the right

In the Paradise Chute

photo **Kenny Biggin** | rider **Scott Muir**

photo **Kenny Biggin** | riders **Doug Bryce, Ewan Moffat, Al Reid**

On top of Bidean. No more Red Bull for you Ewan!

 skimountain

photo **Kenny Biggin** | rider **Doug Bryce**

71. Lost Plot Couloir

harder than: Rustlers

Also known as PDO Gully, this is a steep and gnarly looking gully that sits to skier's left of the Lost Valley Minor Buttress. The route may or may not have been skied from the top but was skied (along with a couple of other lines) from the bergschrund by George Paton et al. in the summer during 1983 or '84. You can find the entrance by following the ridge towards Bidean from the col – the gully entrance is after the first minor summit on the ridge, and is usually corniced and steep.

There are also a couple of other serious lines in this neck of the woods that would require good snow cover and as far as is known haven't seen descents yet.

72. Bealach Dearg

harder than: Lost Bowl

At the head of the Lost Valley, the Bealach Dearg (the red col) provides the route onto the long ridge that links Bidean nam Bian with Stob Coire Sgreamhach. After walking or skinning along the North side of the chasm above the Lost Valley, at the end of the chasm there is the opportunity to trend to the left across a couple of burns. From here it is possible to skin up towards the col but beware of avalanche conditions and cornice/rockfall dangers from above. The headwall will usually be too steep to skin all the way, so crampons and axe are sometimes required. The skiing here can be a little steeper than expected, and it is often well worth a little extra effort to go all the way to the top of Bidean to ski Paradise instead.

73. Bidean Traverses

This is more of a concept than a single route, but one of the best ways to ski routes on the Bidean massif in general is to do one of the many variations of a traverse. Some examples include coming up the Lost Valley, up Bealach Dearg onto the ridge, over Bidean towards Stob Coire nam Beith and down the Massacre Face or even Summit Gully. Or perhaps up Stob Coire nan Lochan and

across to Bidean via its North Ridge and down Paradise into the Lost Valley. Or even up the Lairig Eilde, over Stob Coire Sgreamhach, along the ridge to Bidean, across to Stob Coire nan Lochan and down the North East Face, Broad Gully, or Ossians. Of course there are many different variations but linking these routes, ridges, summits, and bowls together in imaginative ways can create some very memorable days out. It goes without saying that this sort of outing requires good awareness of varying aspects and how the snow conditions are likely to change en route.

photo **Kenny Biggin** | rider **Scott Muir**

The skin in to Bidean with record amounts of snow

Invented in Norway

Powered by you.
Technology by us.

The Rottefella Freeride binding provides
you with optimal grip from edge to edge and
excellent control on hard and icy surfaces.

mountainboot.co.uk

Stob Coire Sgreamhach

The Eastern most and perhaps least well known peak of the Bidean nam Bian massif, Stob Coire Sgreamhach is none the less a fantastic mountain. In addition to the shapely ridge that links it to Bidean, it has the long and spectacular ridge of Beinn Fhada stretching to the North East as well as an often forgotten about corrie to the East. There are in fact many potential lines on Sgreamhach that have not been listed in detail below, and no doubt there is a rich seam of new descents here for those looking for exploration. Unfortunately the otherwise excellent skiing on Sron na Lairig (to the South East) and Beinn Fhada all lies above two nasty chasms that are less than inviting features to ski above, so these routes haven't been included despite the fact that in the right conditions there is a lot of potential here.

Access

The most straightforward way up onto Stob Coire Sgreamhach is via the Lost Valley and up onto the Bealach Dearg that divides Sgreamhach from Bidean. From the col the ridge onto the summit is fairly straightforward.

The alternative approach is one of the harder access routes in the book, both in terms of distance and terrain. Park at the Big Cairn car park as for the Wee Buachaille. From there follow the good path and fairly quickly fork right to cross the Allt Lairig Eilde. The path follows the burn on the West

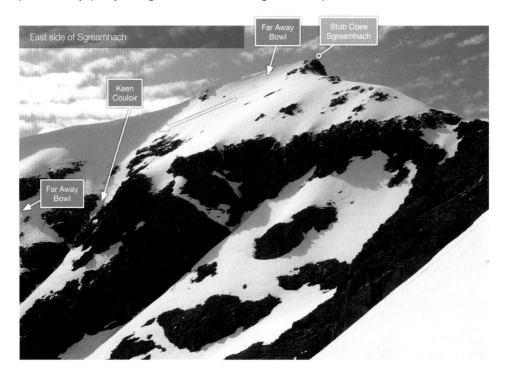

East side of Sgreamhach

Far Away Bowl

Stob Coire Sgreamhach

Keen Couloir

Far Away Bowl

bank for around 1.5km and before crossing back over the burn you should strike out to the West into the large Coir' Eilde. Stay high above the steep chasm and pick your way through a number of rock bands on sometimes precarious ground. The steep sided gorge is known as the Lairig Chasm which was only fairly recently discovered as an ice climbing venue. Once above the gorge the corrie opens out and the remaining skin up to the col on the Beinn Fhada Ridge (Grid Ref: NN157538) is a bit more relaxed. To the left of the col there is the Bad Step – a wall of rock which you either need to skirt below or scramble up to gain the ridge proper. Above the Bad Step the ridge is straightforward to the summit and for the right party, this route up is actually a very worthwhile winter outing in its own right.

74. Slanty Mhath

When the North Face of Sgreamhach is loaded up with snow, there are a number of possible ways down the face (few others of which are known to have been skied), but perhaps the most aesthetically pleasing and interesting line follows a diagonal snow field across the face. This prominent route (pronounced Slanty-Va, a play on the gaelic 'slainte mhath' which means good health) can be clearly seen when looking up into the Lost Valley from the road, and great views of it from Bidean and Stob Coire nan Lochan meant that it was only a matter of time before it caught the attention of freeriders.

The route needs a good awareness of where you are on the face as you don't want to end up getting cliffed out by mistake. Find the entrance a little lower to skier's left of the summit cairn. Initially a gully leads down with some crags on your right. Immediately below these cliffs, hang right below them onto the main diagonal snow field. Follow the snow across the face and drop down a wide gully line that leads you onto more open slopes above the top of the Lost Valley Chasm.

Author's Note: I skied this line with Al Reid and Ewan Moffat after a chance meeting (along with Doug Bryce after they'd skied Boomerang) on top of Bidean nam Bian. The Scottish backcountry scene is definitely on the ascendancy and chance encounters like this seem to become more commonplace all the time. Just before he skied into the top of the line Ewan dropped into conversation the fact that he was 'taking it easy' since he was due to get a hernia operation the next day!

photo **Kenny Biggin**

Some great lines on the North West of Beinn Fhada, but note the major terrain trap below

photo **Kenny Biggin**

Slanty Mhath (and other lines) on the North Face of Sgreamhach

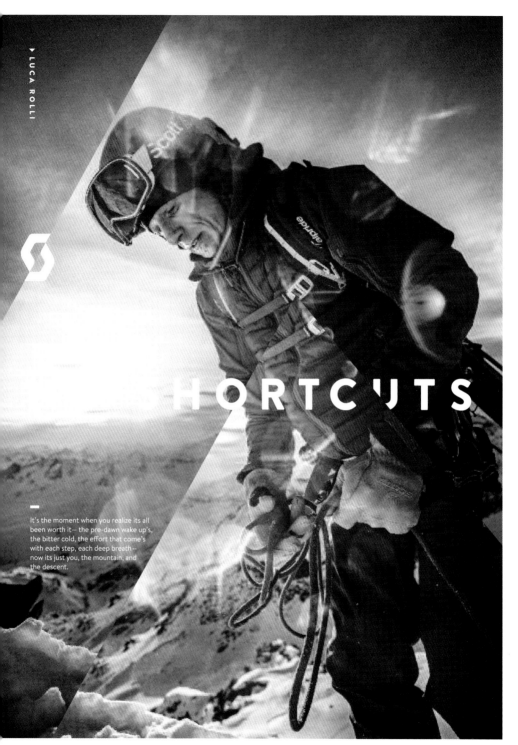

▶ LUCA ROLLI

SHORTCUTS

It's the moment when you realize its all been worth it— the pre-dawn wake up's, the bitter cold, the effort that come's with each step, each deep breath— now its just you, the mountain, and the descent.

Slanty Mhath

Kenny Biggin. Rider Ewan Moffat.

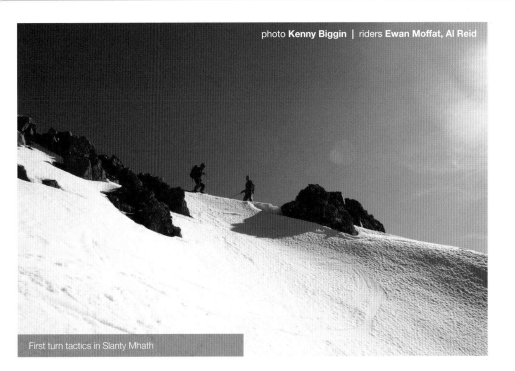

First turn tactics in Slanty Mhath

Getting into the sunshine beyond the ramp on Slanty Mhath

 skimountain

In amongst the North Face of Sgreamhach with the Lost Valley down below

photo **Kenny Biggin** | rider **Al Reid**

75. Fhada Col

2

| harder than: | Lost Bowl |
| combine with: | Diamond Col |

Beinn Fhada is the eastern-most of the Three Sisters and it makes for quite a spectacular ridge in its own right. For the mountaineers amongst you, approaching Stob Coire Sgreamhach along this ridge makes a fine alpine outing. From the skiing perspective there are quite a number of potential routes running along the North West side of Beinn Fhada. However, these don't generally accumulate snow very well and what's worse is that they all lie above the nasty gorge that lurks above the Lost Valley. That isn't to say there isn't some great skiing to be had here (there is) but good conditions are rare and the terrain trap below is fairly off-putting, even if only because it makes the route out quite tricky.

One route on Beinn Fhada that is worthwhile (and less exposed) is the ski down from the col which sits to skier's right of the Bad Step on the ridge. This is a good option for those in the Lost Valley looking for a second run, or for those who have approached via Lairig Eilde who don't fancy continuing on up the ridge to the summit. The advantage of this route over others on Beinn Fhada is that it lies at the Southern end of the chasm below, so skiing to your left to avoid that feature is easy.

76. Far Away Bowl

harder than: Bealach Dearg

The name Stob Coire Sgreamhach means the Peak of the Fearful Corrie, and although it isn't clear which corrie is being referred to, it seems likely to be Coir' Eilde to the East. This route drops into the part of Coir' Eilde (pronounced 'curah-A-lee') closest to the summit, and the reasons behind it being called the Far Away Bowl will no doubt become apparent to those who walk or skin in to this corrie along the Lairig Eilde. Despite the slight trek to get in and out of this corrie, there is some excellent skiing to be had here in a quiet and unvisited location. The route described here follows an interesting but not too difficult line that goes directly from the summit of Stob Coire Sgreamhach.

From the summit cairn you need to do a few turns onto the face, and then traverse quite a long way to your right until you are past the cliffs below you. The ground isn't difficult here but falling wouldn't be a great idea at the top unless the snow is very forgiving. A less exposed but steeper route in would be to go further down the South East Ridge first, but here the cornices can be quite off-putting. Once past the traverse, ski the top of the gully that leads into the Keen Couloir, but head across to skier's right again before getting channelled in. From here the route opens out nicely into

How narrow is too narrow? The Keen Couloir with the Lairig Chasm down below

photo Kenny Biggin

△▲ **ski**mountain

the corrie. Stop and wait for your buddies on the flattening out of the firing line and away from the top of the gorge below.

To skier's right of the Far Away Bowl, the Sron na Lairig plays host to some high quality lines, most of which sit ominously above the Lairig Chasm and no descents here are known of to date.

77. Keen Couloir

harder than: Far Away Bowl

Slap bang in the middle of the Far Away Bowl, is a long and narrow slot that needs lots of snow to be wide enough to ski. Reach the top of the gully as for the Far Away Bowl, and then drop down into the guts of the gully keeping your fingers crossed that it is wide enough. The gully feature is actually the headwaters of the Allt Lairig Eilde and an extension of the far more severe chasm down below at the foot of the corrie.

Author's Note: I can confirm that the narrow part of the Keen Couloir is around 175cm wide as one of my 185cm skis got well and truly wedged stuck on my way down, causing a five minute faffing and swearing session followed by an annoying three step down climb before being able to get my skis back on. Therefore I would highly recommend this gully to those with either short skis or a penchant for straight lining things.

The top of the Far Away Bowl

photo **Kenny Biggin** | rider **Scott Aston**

Scottish Offpiste: Nevis Range & Ben Nevis

Also available in all good bookshops

photo **Kenny Biggin** | rider **Neil Muir**

Skiing off the summit of Aonach Beag at the start of the South Face.

your way between the rock band on skins is reasonably doable. Many will need to take skis off to get through the rocks.

Continue up the ridge staying well away from the big cornices that form on the left (East) side. The summit area in particular is known for forming huge cornices so stay well away from the edge. Take ... some photos and then ski back!

...healaich Face

4   **harder than:**   Chancers

...ariety of lines down the North Face of Stob Coire Bhealaich – these lie in between the ...marked 1090 and 1048 on the 1:25000 map. You get a great view of this face if you

Stob Coire Bhealaich   Martini Couloir   Aonach Beag
SCB Col   Bhealaich Face   Calm Couloir   Rough Couloir

photo **Kenny Biggin**

59. Rough Couloir

3   **harder than:** Summit Gully   **combine with:** The Grey Corries

This is a fantastic long couloir taking you down almost 600metres of great skiing into remote backcountry. The name comes from the gaelic for this face which is An Aghaidh Gharbh – The Ro... Face. The cornice at the top will often be big and any avalanches coming off the steep East Face above funnel into here so tread carefully. From the summit of Aonach Beag, ski down southwards around 100metres of height loss keeping the big cornices on your left – this in itself can be a nice s...

When the gradient eases the entrance is on your left – the best place to look in is usually on a small rise on the right of the entrance. There are a choice of ways in. The top third is reasonably open before everything funnels into a walled gully. After a while things open up again and there is an opportunity to take a rest in a safer spot over to the right.

Below here the gully closes in again for the bottom third and it takes quite a lot of snow to fill this in as there are a couple of steep sections – if you don't fancy staying in the guts of the gully there is easier skiing down the right to the corrie floor.

Looking into the Rough Couloir

122 | Aonach Beag   © SkiMou...

Aonach Eagach

Stretching along the North side of Glencoe all the way from the Devil's Staircase at Altnafeadh to the Pap of Glencoe (Sgorr na Ciche), a long ridge stands opposite the opposing mass of Bidean nam Bian. The central part of this chain forms one of the most famous ridges in the country – the Aonach Eagach. At first glance the skiing on this side of the glen is fairly limited, however there are a few hidden gems in amongst these mountains, especially for those who are looking for something different.

The best skiing lies over the back in the Northerly bowls where there are several large corries. Even on the North side however, there is only quite limited ski potential coming off the main ridge – there is the odd steep gully line, but often the terrain is complex and the lines are too short to be real classics anyway. The main longer gully potential lies on the North West flank of Meall Dearg where there are at least a couple of nice looking lines, given good snow cover (a rope may well be required). The routes described below are the more obvious candidates, though other lines are no doubt available to those who seek them out.

Gnarly ground on the South side of Aonach Eagach   photo **Kenny Biggin**

78. Stob Mhic Mhartuin

starting height:	310m
summit height:	707m
start:	Paraffin Lizzie's

This small hill marks the eastern end of the Aonach Eagach ridge system. On its own it makes a great little outing on a day when both the snow and cloud are low down. Since the starting point at Paraffin Lizzie's car park is also pretty much the highest point of the road, when the snow is lying low it is often possible to put your skins on beside the road. Since it is low and South facing, the snow on this slope often doesn't stay around for long. The route follows a gentle slope in amongst heathery knolls and stream systems and soon brings you onto the broad ridge that leads to the summit. Head to the right of the crags that lie at the summit where a few kick turns up the only steeper pitch will take you onto the summit plateau. To descend, either retrace your skin track to the East and then down, or drop off the summit to skier's right (West) of the crags which can give some nice skiing but will leave you with a short walk back up the road to finish. If the weather clears up while you're up there why not continue up onto the main ridge?

Author's Note: The car park is named after the food van that used to be parked here, hosted by its namesake Liz, which served rolls that tasted distinctly of the stove's fuel.

The easy summit of Stob Mhic Mhartuin   photo **Kenny Biggin**

79. The Easy Eagach

starting height:	310m
summit height:	903m
start:	Paraffin Lizzie's

Despite its proximity to the much harder Aonach Eagach, the section of ridge between the Devil's Staircase and Am Bodach is far more gentle, open, and accessible. This is a nice and relatively easy ridge top tour from a high(ish) starting point with a choice of descent options. You can start this tour at either end, but easiest from a skinning point of view is to start at the East end as for Stob Mhic Mhartuin. From the top of Stob Mhic Mhartuin continue West onto the main ridge at Sron a'Choire Odhair-bhig. More leisurely skinning takes you onto the top marked 903 and then on round to Sron Garbh. You can optionally continue on from here to Am Bodach which is where the difficulties of the Aonach Eagach start.

There are a variety of options for descent from the Easy Eagach – the two big burn lines – Allt Coire Meannarclach and Allt Ruigh – on the South side are good when there is snow down to the road, and both these lines take you back within reasonable hitchhiking distance to get back to your car. The more adventurous alternative routes drop down the Northern side of the ridge and all of these suddenly take you into quite remote feeling terrain. There are three large North facing corries here – Coire Odhar-mor on the East end, Coire Mhorair in the middle, and Coire nan Lab at the West end. All three of these corries offer some great skiing of varying gradients and aspects and hold their snow reasonably well.

Having dropped into one of these Northern bowls, the task of extricating yourself becomes apparent – from Coire nan Lab the easiest way out is either to skin back up and over to the road, or even traverse West across flat ground to drop into Gleann a' Chaolais which (lower down) has a path of sorts on the North bank of the burn which leads to the road at the side of Loch Leven. Dropping into the other two corries the options are to either skin back up and over, or ski as best you can out to your right with the aim of joining the West Highland Way. Once on the West Highland Way, it can either be followed down into Kinlochleven (around 3km) or back over and down beside the Devil's Staircase – neither are short options but they may appeal to the expeditionaries amongst you. The snow conditions and your propensity for touring over flattish ground will dictate which option appeals most.

Looking West from halfway along the Aonach Eagach Traverse

80. The Aonach Eagach Traverse

| harder than: | Bidean & Buchaille Traverses |
| combine with: | The Easy Eagach |

The Aonach Eagach is the impressive stretch of ridge that lies between Am Bodach and Stob Coire Leith. The Gaelic Aonach Eagach translates as 'notched ridge' and it certainly lives up to its name. Although there is some very limited steep skiing potential on the South side which faces Glencoe, chief amongst these being Farm Gully or Big Boulder Gully (no known ski descents), really the side of the mountain facing the road is far too steep and craggy, and not snow sure enough to offer good skiing. In fact there are frequent rescue team call outs for people who have tried to descend off the ridge to the South and the ground here is treacherous and best avoided.

The traverse of the ridge is a classic scrambling outing in summer and a worthy (climbing grade II) mountaineering trip in full winter conditions. For ski mountaineers, the ridge offers a great winter or spring traverse, but to be honest the trip is a bit of a novelty act with skis as realistically there won't be much skiing on the actual ridge, while there is likely to be a lot of clattering skis off rocks. No doubt there are those of you out there who will still enjoy tackling the outing and of course it is a nice thing to have done in retrospect.

Skiing off Stob Coire Leith with the back of Aonach Eagach above

The best route up onto the ridge is to park at the Sand Pit car park and follow the path up towards Am Bodach. If there is lots of snow you will be able to start skinning into Coire an Ruigh which will take you onto the ridge coming from Sron Garbh. Heading West from Am Bodach the difficulties start immediately with a tricky descent. The ridge between Am Bodach and Meall Dearg provides a taste of things to come and for those who reach Meall Dearg finding it hard, now is the time to either retrace your steps or descend into one of the Northern corries from there.

From Meall Dearg the main difficulties start and a series of pinnacles need some awkward scrambling where a short rope may well help with confidence. By the time you reach Stob Coire Leith you are likely to be gagging to put your skis on your feet, and one of the best descent options drops down the North East Face into the corrie. There are spectacular views from here back up at the complex North side of the ridge. Follow the burn as far as the snow allows and aim to end up on the North side of it where a broken path leads down Gleann a' Chaolais to the road where hopefully you had the foresight to leave a car (Grid Ref: NN143608).

A tricky section on the Aonach Eagach traverse with Loch Achtriochtan below

photo Kenny Biggin | rider Nigel Wombell

Aonach Eagach from Stob Coire nan Lochan

Looking into Sgorr nam Fiannaidh's Northern corrie

81. Sgorr nam Fiannaidh

combine with: Aonach Eagach Traverse

The Western end of the Aonach Eagach has the highest summit and probably actually the best skiing. The best route up starts from almost sea level so offers you little in the way of a high car park, but the quality of the remote bowl on the far side is well worth the trek. This is also a route that it is possible to sneak up when the snow gates are closed on the main road, so long as you are stranded on the North side of them. The best way to do this trip is with two cars, leaving one of them on the Kinlochleven road at Caolasnacon (Grid Ref: NN141607). Having done a car shuttle, start from the backroad between Glencoe village and the Clachaig where there is a path leading up through the trees signed to the Pap of Glencoe (Grid Ref: NN111586). Branch off the Pap path to the right after a short climb and head laboriously up towards Sgorr nam Fiannaidh's broad North West Ridge. For those with a peak bagging mindset, a detour across to take in the Pap is an option even if just for the views as it doesn't generally accumulate enough snow to make for a good skiing venue.

The best skiing from Sgorr nam Fiannaidh is into the large Coire Corcaig to the North East. There are multiple options route wise into this corrie, including entrances suitable for most tastes, but down the North East Face directly from the summit is likely to be the most popular choice and this offers a good long descent into a wild-feeling bowl. On your way out of the corrie, aim to stay on the right bank of the burn away from the gorge, and (if there is enough snow) heading onto the shoulder on the right is a good bet.

If you only have one car, you could also ascend via Sgorr nam Fiannaidh's North Ridge from Caolasnacon. Of course, it is also well worth considering continuing across to Sgorr nam Fiannaidh from Stob Coire Leith after doing the Aonach Eagach traverse.

Sgorr Dhearg

Sgorr Dhearg marks the Western edge of this guidebook area. The mountain sits on a ridge with its sister mountain Sgorr Dhonuill and together they make up Beinn a' Bheithir (which translates as Mountain of the Thunderbolt). While there are a number of routes worthy of skiing on these hills, the most appealing and accessible from an offpiste skier's perspective is the North Eastern corrie (Coire Giubhsachain) of Sgorr Dhearg. This large corrie is only just visible from the road – you can get a glimpse up into it as you're driving South towards the Ballachulish Bridge and again as you whizz past St John's church outside Ballachulish. The best view of the corrie however, is gained by driving a short distance down the road on the North side of Loch Leven and it is well worth taking this detour to assess snow cover before heading up there.

82. Spring Bowl

combine with: Fin Chute

So named because the snow clings on in this corrie long after most of the rest of Beinn a' Bheithir begins to look bare. This trip makes an excellent spring outing with no real difficulties other than the long walk in. Unfortunately there is no high car park so light touring kit is the order of the day. Start by going under the Ballachulish Bridge on the Oban road, go past the hotel and turn left just after the golf course following the signs to the forest walks. Park at the Gleann a' Chaolais (pronounced 'glen-a-hoolish') forestry car park (Grid Ref: NN048590). Follow the forest track for half a kilometre and turn left to cross over the bridge. Then follow the track and path through the forest to the South which climbs up to around 500metres. From where the path leaves the forest it is sometimes possible to put skins on and go across the flat bottom of the corrie before climbing up the headwall (not steep) between some rocks up on to the col between Sgorr Dhonuill and Sgorr Dhearg at Grid Ref: NN048554.

The ridge up onto Sgorr Dhearg from the col is easy and the view into the bowl you've come to ski is a great reward for your efforts so far. Now all you have to do is flick your boots into ski mode and choose a line to ski. The easiest options are to go down the ridge a little way to the East where there are lots of nice entrances into the bowl. Having gone to the effort of getting here, the corrie is crying out for you to do two laps – one in the bowl, and one down Fin Chute (see the next route description for the route out).

BEINN A BHEITHIR

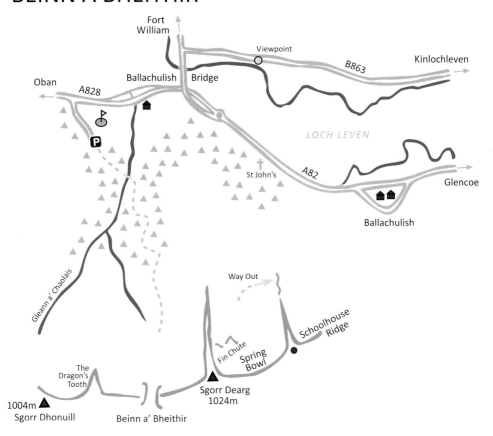

Fort William

Viewpoint

Kinlochleven

B863

Oban

A828

Ballachulish

Bridge

LOCH LEVEN

St John's

A82

Glencoe

Ballachulish

Gleann a' Chaolais

Way Out

Schoolhouse Ridge

Fin Chute

Spring Bowl

The Dragon's Tooth

Sgorr Dearg
1024m

1004m
Sgorr Dhonuill

Beinn a' Bheithir

Beinn a' Bheithir

photo **Kenny Biggin**

83. Fin Chute

2

harder than: Spring Bowl

The setting of this line is close to perfection – you can ski right from the summit, carving your line beside the picturesque rock fin, with the view behind of Loch Linnhe and Loch Leven being nothing short of spectacular.

Having patted yourself on the back for skiing a great line, you now need to find your way down. Ski down the corrie and burn line as far as the snow allows. Probably the best way out is to do this route when there is enough snow to traverse out of the corrie to skier's right, over Beinn Bhan and ski down the slopes above Ballachulish (West Laroch). There is also a route down through the trees towards St John's church – the old path starts at a stile to skier's right of the burn at the treeline, but it can be tricky to find.

If you're determined to get back to your car without having to hitch you can try going to the left of the corrie over the ridge above Meall a' Chaolais. However, from here pick your route carefully – there is a very rough firebreak through the trees which leads eventually down to meet the forest track, but if you get it wrong the day may become memorable for all the wrong bushwhacking reasons.

There are a number of other inviting looking skiing options here, including approaching via the classic Schoolhouse Ridge, or from Glen Duror, or perhaps skiing a line or two directly above Ballachulish.

Wintery possibilities above Ballachulish

photo **Kenny Biggin**

Skinning up Stob Coire nan Lochan with the Ballachulish Bridge and Spring Bowl behind

Sunshine, snow, and a great line on Sgorr Dhearg

photo **Kenny Biggin** | rider **Ian Lloyd**

No snow left apart from the 500metre descent below in Spring Bowl

photo **Kenny Biggin** | rider **Ian Lloyd**

Parking for Sgorr Dhearg

photo **Kenny Biggin**

What a line – beside the Fins on Sgorr Dhearg, Loch Linnhe & Loch Leven below

photo **Kenny Biggin** | rider **Ian Lloyd**

Bridge of Orchy & Tyndrum Hills

Sitting at the Southern end of this guidebook area there are some fantastic mountains offering a prelude to the entry to Glencoe proper. As you travel North of Loch Lomond and beyond through the villages of Crianlarich and Tyndrum, there is a definite feeling of having entered the Highlands with all the wildness and opportunity that brings. Although the main two mountains focused on here are Ben Lui and Beinn an Dothaidh, bear in mind that both of these hills have a number of neighbours all of which have excellent skiing potential. Note that these hills are featured on a different map to most of the rest of the book – the OS 1:50,000 Sheet 50, Glen Orchy & Loch Etive is probably most useful here.

The Bridge of Orchy hills at their best, from Rubicon Ridge on Meall a' Bhuiridh

84. Tyndrum Faces

As you climb up the road out of Tyndrum in the depths of winter, there are a couple of similar long and uniform slopes just crying out for ski tracks. The most obvious of these are the broad South Ridge of Beinn Odhar and the Fuaran Mor that drops from the top of Beinn Dorain. Despite how good they can look on occasion, they are rarely skied - perhaps because you are always on your way somewhere else. The easiest to stop and do is Beinn Odhar – you can park and get across the railway just North of Tyndrum at Grid Ref: NN332318. From here skin up into Coire Thoin and on up to the summit. The slope back to the car faces almost due South so rarely holds good snow for long, so if you see it looking good make the most of it. Note that several of the slopes around here have been known to avalanche and block the railway.

CREATING FOOTWEAR FOR ALL ALTITUDES,
IN ANY CONDITIONS

Beinn an Dothaidh

Driving South after a great ski at Meall a' Bhuiridh, it is almost impossible to miss the skiing potential offered by the great North face of Beinn an Dothaidh. Pronounced 'Bine Doe-ay' (and frequently just 'Ben Doh'), this is just one of a number of great hills that sit above Bridge of Orchy - Beinn Dorain, Beinn Achaladair, and Beinn a Chreachain are all worthy candidates for ski tours. Although there is unquestionably good skiing on the other hills, for the offpiste skier Beinn an Dothaidh offers the easiest access coupled with some brilliant descents.

Access

There are two main options for approaching Beinn an Dothaidh – you can park at the train station car park which is found up the little road opposite the Bridge of Orchy Hotel; or you can park at the edge of Loch Tulla in a gravel car park a short way up the track leading towards Achallader Farm. From Bridge of Orchy station, go through the underpass and up onto the good path that follows the Allt Coire an Dothaidh. With luck you will have your skins on fairly quickly and progress up to the col in between Beinn an Dothaidh and Beinn Dorain is relatively easy going. There are great views from the col across to the massive easy bowl below Beinn Dorain and for those wanting easy terrain this area is perfect. For those heading up to the main event, skin up the ridge to the North and then continue across the open plateau to one of the two main summits.

If approaching from the North side, bash more or less straight up the slope from the car park and carefully cross the railway. If there is no snow it can be wet and boggy going across the ground above but with snow and skins it is quite a pleasant route. Head around the East side of the ridge that drops down from the summit. Here there is an obvious landmark in the shape of a small knoll known as the Fairy's Hat which stands separate from the main ridge (Grid Ref: NN327418). Cut to skinner's right of this up a short and easy gully which takes you to a great vantage point to take a look at the North Face lines as well as up into West Gully and the Fairy Bowl.

If you have two cars it makes a nice trip to approach from Bridge of Orchy and ski down the far side to Achallader. When there is enough snow the ski across the heather down towards Achallader is great fun.

An end of season West Gully foray   photo **Neil Muir** | rider **Kenny Biggin**

Taking advantage of roadside snow on the way into Beinn an Dothaidh from Achallader

photo **Kenny Biggin** | rider **Neil Muir**

△skimountain

BEINN AN DOTHAIDH

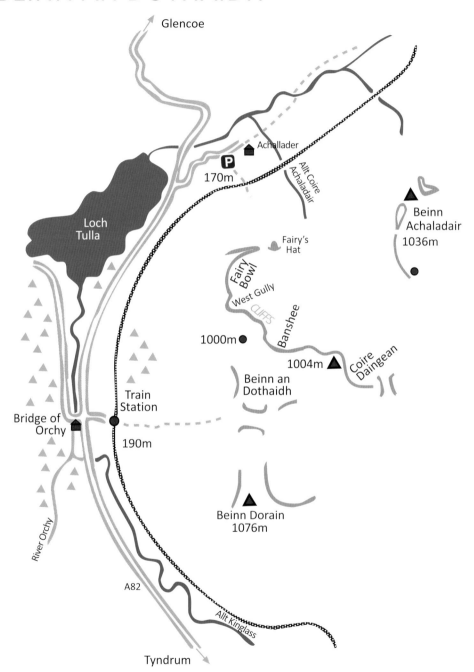

Glencoe

Achallader

P
170m

Allt Coire Achaladair

Loch Tulla

Beinn Achaladair
1036m

Fairy's Hat

Fairy Bowl

West Gully

CLIFFS

Banshee

1000m

1004m

Coire Daingean

Beinn an Dothaidh

Train Station
190m

Bridge of Orchy

River Orchy

Beinn Dorain
1076m

A82

Allt Kinglass

Tyndrum

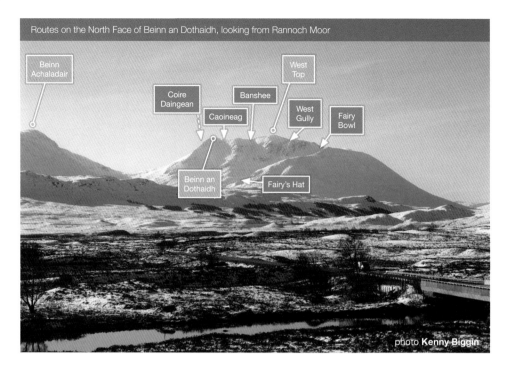

Beinn Achaladair

West Top

Coire Daingean

Banshee

Caoineag

West Gully

Fairy Bowl

Beinn an Dothaidh

Fairy's Hat

photo **Kenny Biggin**

85. Fairy Bowl

1-2

similar to:	Diamond Col
combine with:	West Gully

The top of this bowl lies at only 900metres, but it provides a fantastic and very accessible way of skiing this mountain without having to do anything serious. There is a wide choice of entries, with further up generally being steeper and more corniced. Multiple laps are the order of the day here as skinning back up is easier than the trek back to the car! Having skied the main bowl, the nicest route down is to follow the stream bed on skier's right as far as the Fairy's Hat – cut to the left of that which puts you on a good line to ski back to the car.

Looking into the Fairy Bowl with West Gully on the left

Scoring some sweet turns in the Fairy Bowl

photo **Neil Muir** | rider **Kenny Biggin**

Kenny getting his moneys worth for the walk-in at the top of West Gully

86. West Gully

harder than: Massacre Face, Local Hero

Also called Hanging Couloir because of the way it sits on the face, West Gully is a cracking route which drops down between big rock walls and it deserves to be skied far more often than it is. You can find the entrance from the top by descending West from Beinn an Dothaidh's West top for around 200metres – the top of the gully is an obvious opening on the ridge and you can get a good look down it if you work your way around the edge. There is often a cornice which can be avoided well out to skier's left.

Last chance to enjoy the sunshine in West Gully

photo Kenny Biggin | rider Neil Muir

photo Kenny Biggin | rider Neil Muir

Spring snow in West Gully

© SkiMountain

87. Banshee

harder than: West Gully

Skier looking small in the guts of Banshee

photo **Kenny Biggin** | rider **Neil Muir**

Around 100metres to skier's right of Beinn an Dothaidh's West top, there is a large and corniced gully entrance. The hardest thing about this route will often be getting in to it, with the easiest entrance being to cut in from skier's right above some small crags. Depending on snow build up there can be a narrowing further down so it is worth checking the route is complete before committing. The route is never extremely steep but is quite sustained and has the feeling of being in a gully in the middle of a big North face (which you are). After several hundred metres the line spills out into the main corrie and you can enjoy opening out for a while before traversing left towards the Fairy's Hat and the route home.

Author's Note: Although no descents are known of, closer to the main summit there is also another steep line (perhaps named 'Caoineag') that cuts down the North face for several hundred metres. This is a more serious line than Banshee next to it as it is steeper, narrower, and rockier. A banshee is a fairy woman who is said to be seen washing the bloodstained clothing of those who are about to die. A caoineag is a similar spirit to a banshee and it is said that prior to the Massacre of Glencoe, the Caoineag of the MacDonalds was heard to wail night after night. While you're lying in bed in the early hours on a snowy weekend, listening to the wind whistling past the window, and anticipating skiing a big route the next day… keep your ears open for a faint wailing that might signal a cautious approach could be in order.

Nice easy entrance into Coire Daingean with mellow skiing on Beinn Dorain in the background

photo **Kenny Biggin**

88. Coire Daingean

2

similar to: Creise Bowl

The easiest way off the mountain on the North side is to drop to the East of the main summit into Coire Daingean. There is a nice wide bowl here with fairly easy angled ground and for many this or the Fairy Bowl will be the routes of choice if doing a tour over the mountain. Having dropped into the corrie it can seem like a fair way back out to the car although there is at least a bit of gradient all the way so long as your skis aren't sticking.

89. Back to the Bridge

The trick is to remember the ski, and forget the walk
photo Kenny Biggin | rider Neil Muir

Although the bulk of the good offpiste skiing is on the North side of the mountain, when the snow is right the skiing on the South and West side is also worthwhile. There is nothing too steep here either so a trip like this is a good option on dodgy avalanche days. From the summit ski gently down the Southern slopes towards the col with Beinn Dorain and then drop into Coire an Dothaidh back towards Bridge of Orchy.

Beinn an Dothaidh and Beinn Achaladair from Rannoch Moor
photo Kenny Biggin

skimountain

Ben Lui

Ben Lui is a classically shaped triangular mountain that stands out on the skyline from many of the mountains that lie to the North in this guidebook. There are several other nice mountains close by which are all well worth a ski, especially Ben Oss and Beinn Dubhchraig which are both accessed from the Cononish, and Ben Challum on the far side of Tyndrum, but the cherry on the cake in this particular area is definitely Ben Lui so that is the focus of this section of the book.

The area around and including Ben Lui has been designated a National Nature Reserve for its exceptionally rich and varied upland plants. For the offpiste skier this doesn't have too many direct implications other than be responsible as you would be elsewhere on the hills – of course you should also keep a look out for the large blue bird that is shown on the OS map as it is very rare to spot it.

Access

The usual routes in are either from Dalrigh just South of Tyndrum, or from the A85 in Glen Lochy. Both have their pros and cons and neither route is an easy option. Crampons and axe may well be required whichever route you go up and this is undoubtedly a real winter expedition so come prepared. The approach from Dalrigh (park at Grid Ref: NN343292) is best in conjunction with a bike. Strap your skis on either to your bag or your bike and follow the track in towards and then past the farm with its green roofs at Cononish. The track gets rougher after the farm but the bikes remain useful until you reach the Allt an Rund at Grid Ref: NN282274, around 6km from Dalrigh. After

Ben Lui from Tyndrum side

photo **Mike Guest**

Ben Lui

Luigi

Central Gully

Bluebird Bowl

Cononish Couloir

BEN LUI

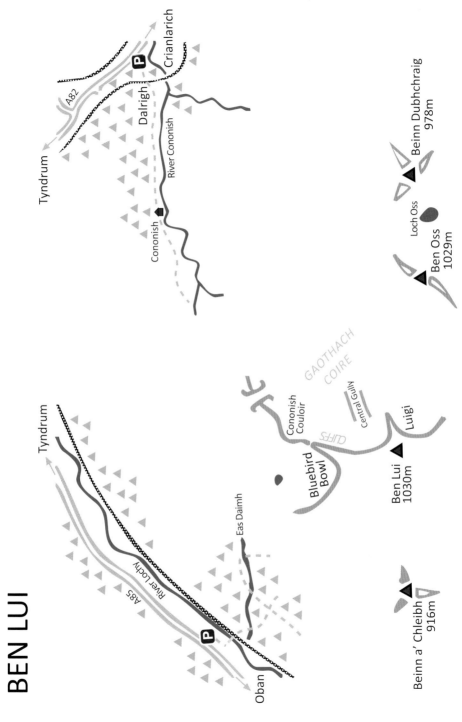

photo **Kenny Biggin** | rider **Brian Morrison**

leaving the bikes, head up into Coire Gaothach, with Ben Lui's big North East Face directly in front of you allowing you to get a good look at your lines. Once in the corrie break out to your right onto the North Ridge and follow this up to the summit, taking note of the various lines on offer on your way.

The alternative approach route is to take a left turn just North of Tyndrum onto the A85 to Oban. After around 10km, turn left into a forestry car park at Grid Ref: NN239278. There is a path leading out of the car park which feels great until you realise it just leads to a river crossing with, at the time of writing, no bridge. Now is the time to call in whatever favours are owed and decide who is carrying who across the river. Once on the far side of the river, dry your feet and stop whimpering before carefully crossing the railway close to where it tells you not to*. A path of sorts leads through some dense forest and some perseverance is required to keep going at this point. Keep following the 'path' until you come to an obvious fork in the burn – take the right hand fork and then cross over to the far right hand bank where the eagle eyed will spot a gate leading to a much better path taking you through the newer part of the forest. Once you reach the forest track, head left until it leads to the Eas Daimh burn and another boggy path that will take you out onto the open hillside at around Grid Ref: NN253275. From here at least you don't have to battle the forest anymore, just your willpower and lack of fitness. Trend up onto Ben Lui's North West Ridge which takes you up to the summit.

*Author's Note: Please note SkiMountain and the author expressly do not encourage people to cross the railway here as it remains dangerous to do so until a nice little footbridge across the river and a level crossing are put in.

photo **Brian Morrison** | rider **Kenny Biggin**

Neil was starting to suspect being a published author was going to Kenny's head

Approaching from Glen Lochy

photo **Kenny Biggin** | riders **Neil Muir, Brian Morrison**

Cycling into Ben Lui via Cononish

photo **Mike Guest** | riders **Al Conroy, Jonny Lonie**

90. Central Gully

   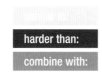

harder than:	Cononish Couloir
combine with:	Bluebird Bowl

Not to be confused with the Central Gully on Bidean nam Bian, this route was one of the first winter climbs recorded in Scotland. This is a highly sought after descent amongst those in the know; although the lengthy approach, large cornices, weather, and snow conditions mean that it only sees skiers infrequently.

The summit of Ben Lui is made up of two tops with the corniced entrance to the North East Face running between them. The best entrance to Central Gully is usually on skier's right of this face. After dropping in, there are a number of turns worth on the large upper snow field before the entrance to the main gully opens up on the left. When there is lots of snow on the face you can also ski a line to the right of the gully as well which will be less exposed to cornice debris from above. The gully itself is narrow and steep, but not unmanageably so. Around a hundred metres of descent in the main gully lead to it opening out into Coire Gaothach where you can GS turn down as far as the snow will allow.

With good snow cover, other lines open up on the main face to skier's left of Central Gully, although

On the North East Face just above Central Gully   photo **Kenny Biggin** | rider **Brian Morrison**

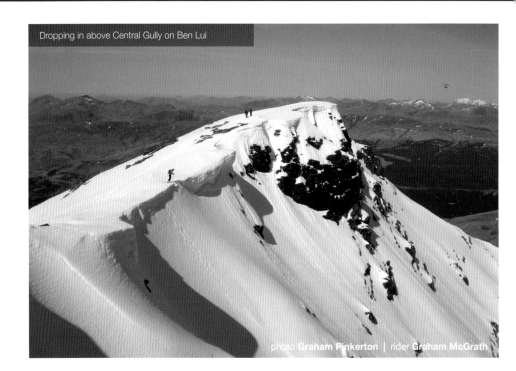

Dropping in above Central Gully on Ben Lui

photo **Graham Pinkerton** | rider **Graham McGrath**

there are several rock outcrops here to be avoided. If cornices above the main face are too off-putting, one option is to sneak onto the face from below the summit cairn which can be skirted around quite easily from skier's right. Following the ridge down below the cairn also leads onto a subsidiary face which may provide an interesting variation to the main event.

In 1932, this was also the location of one of the earliest recorded avalanche incidents. As described in the classic Scottish avalanche book 'A Chance in a Million?', four climbers survived here after sliding almost the entire length of the face. Taking place on the 12th of May, this shows how late in the season incidents can occur.

91. Cononish Couloir

| similar to: | Paradise |
| combine with: | Bluebird Bowl |

Around two thirds of the way up Ben Lui's North Ridge on skier's left of Coire Gaothach, this gully provides a great consolation prize for those who don't fancy the look of Central Gully. If skiing it from the summit it is possible to ski the top turns of Bluebird Bowl before breaking out right onto the ridge to get to the entrance of the Cononish Couloir. Although shorter in comparison to the main face, this is still a nice ski and well worth a trip in its own right.

photo & rider **Mike Guest**

At the top of the Cononish Couloir

92. Bluebird Bowl

similar to:	Creise Bowl
combine with:	Central Gully

This is one of those routes that turns an already attractive mountain into a perfect freeride destination. Not only does Ben Lui have its big North East Face, but right next to it there is this extremely pleasant and accessible North facing bowl suitable for the majority of offpiste skiers. From the North West top of the summit, there are a variety of easy entrance options and although the top few turns are a little steeper, this soon eases out allowing you to do long fast turns down towards the small lochan that sits in the corrie forming the headwaters of the River Cononish. From the lochan the corrie goes over a rise before continuing down, and when there is enough snow there is a good long descent to be had here heading down towards skier's right aiming for the Allt an Rund in the glen below. If you have left your bikes at the top of the Cononish track, a traverse along to the right will take you back towards where you left them. Alternatively, if you are heading back to the Glen Lochy side you can trend over to skier's left, being careful to avoid the steeper craggy ground on your way back to the top of the Eas Daimh path through the forest.

photo **Kenny Biggin** | rider **Neil Muir**

Lining up for the run home into Bluebird Bowl

93. Luigi

harder than: Bluebird Bowl

Another route well worth skiing is the Eastern bowl that drops down immediately to skier's right of the summit cairn. If the North East Face looks a bit too dramatic for you, this may well be a more suitable option. The ground is more open here and although the fall-line takes you slightly in the wrong direction, if the snow is low enough you can ski for 5-600 metres before traversing out to the left back towards the head of the Cononish track. It is also worth noting that if the snow isn't all that low, you may prefer to ski the top part of Luigi, but then cut across below a band of cliffs to cross over the minor col on the East Ridge which will give you access back into the main corrie.

Pronunciation & Translations

Even for the author who grew up just outside Fort William, pronunciation of some of the names encountered on a map of the area can be tricky at best. Hopefully the following will provide enough of an idiots' guide to be able at least to read the book without getting stuck. Perhaps it is also worth a quick explanation of some of the less widely known Scottish words for those of you who are flocking to sample Scotland's offpiste wonders from abroad – a burn is a small river or stream, while a loch is a Scottish lake (a lochan is a small loch), and a glen is a valley.

Pronunciation of Tricky Words

Name	Pronunciation	Notes
Meall a' Bhuiridh	Myowl-a-Voorey	'Bh' in Gaelic is a 'v' sound. Meall is often pronounced 'meal' but 'myowl' is more accurate. ('l', 'n', and 'r' are the only letters that can be doubled and they change the preceding vowel sound)
Clach Leathad	Clach-let	Pronounce ch as a guttural sound as in Loch, not as in Chicken, nor as in Lock. Note that 'th' in Gaelic is silent in the middle of words (and 'th' is an 'h' sound at the start of words).
Bidean	Beej-an	Often pronounced (even by many locals) exactly as it looks, but more correctly pronounced 'beejan'. 'D' next to 'i' or 'e' gives a 'j' sound as in Bidean and Dearg.
Coire (or Choire)	Coruh	The English translation of these is just 'corrie', but the gaelic sounds more like 'coruh'. The 'ch' in choire is pronounced in Gaelic as in loch.
Ballachulish	Bal-a-hoolish	
Dubh / Dhubh	Doo / Goo	Dubh and dhubh are not quite the same. Dubh is pronounced a bit like 'doo' but dhubh is more like 'goo'. Farther variations include dhuibh - all of these indicate variations in meaning, gender, etc.
Glas / Ghlais	Glass / Ghlash	The 'gh' is a bit like 'ch' in loch, but with a 'g' start to it. The variations are often due to case changes – e.g. Coire Glas = Grey Corrie. Allt a' Choire Ghlais (Burn of the Grey Corrie). 'I' or 'e' next to the letter 's' gives you the English 'sh' sound.
Beinn a' Bheithir	Bine-a-Vair	In Gaelic Beinn is pronounced roughly 'bine' but the very common Anglicisation of the word is just 'ben'.
Beinn an Dothaidh	Bine Doe-ay	Frequently pronounced simply 'Ben Doe' – probably since a lot of the early hill walkers in the Highlands were ship yard workers who were partly deaf from riveting.
Odhar / odhair	Oor	One that catches many people out, there are yet more silent letters in this word

There are many other less than obvious Gaelic words throughout this book, and where possible they are accompanied by a rough guide to their pronunciation.

Gaelic Words

As you look across the map of Glencoe there are a fairly small selection of words that appear time and again. With a rudimentary understanding of what some of the words mean, some of the names you see will start to make (a little) sense. In fact the names can sometimes give you some clues as to what sort of terrain you are likely to come across.

Gaelic	Rough Translation
Bealach	A col on a ridge
Sron	Nose - often a prominent ridge feature
Stob / Meall / Creag / Carn / Sgurr / Bidean / Beinn	Various sorts and shapes of hill, peak, or mountain. Roughly the breakdown is: stob = point; meall = rounded hill; creag = crag; carn = stony hill; sgurr = jagged peak; bidean = conical peak; beinn = any mountain or hill, but often a big one.
Allt / Abhainn	Burn (or stream) / River
Eas / easan / easain	Waterfall or rapid. Eas is a waterfall, plural easan, but easan can also mean a little waterfall.
Drochaid	Bridge
Aonach / Druim / Leathad	Ridges (Aonach is a high ridge while Leathad is a broad one, Leathad can also mean slope)
Eagach	Notched
Beag / Mor	Small / Big
Dubh / Ban / Dearg / Ghlais / Odhar / Buidhe	Colours: dubh = black, ban = white, dearg = red, ghlais = grey, odhar = dun-coloured (brownish), buidhe = yellow
Fada / Gearr	Long / Short
Lairig	A low glen or pass

The First Maps

There must have been some mighty confusion caused back in the days when the names we now see on maps were used more descriptively in everyday conversation. The following conversation may have taken place somewhere in Glencoe, circa 1650 (in Gaelic):

Hector: "Right then Tavish, that's me off... I'm going to take the cattle on up to the dun coloured corrie next to the grey corrie with the wee black burn in it."

Tavish: "OK laddie, I'll bring the peat in and then come and meet you up there. Do you mean the grey corrie next to the ridge with the heather on it or the other one next to the dun coloured hill?"

Hector [looking back over his shoulder, already almost out of earshot]: "Aye, that's the one. Near where the hill with the roaring stags is, you know the one."

Tavish [muttering to himself]: "I bet he goes somewhere completely different again and I spend the next three days looking for him... there are stags roaring on pretty much all of the hills at this time of year and none of us even knows what colour 'dun' actually is! Next he'll be naming glens after the flipping midgies. Ach well, I'll write these names down on this new 'map' thingy anyway... give it a few centuries and I suppose they'll work out what we meant."

Mountain Stats

One of the features that makes this area great as an offpiste skiing destination is the density of high mountains. For interest, the table below provides an impression of the high Scottish peaks within a relatively small area… and of course the majority of these lie very close to one of the highest roads in the country.

Mountain (in height order)	Height (m)	Official Munro
Stob Coire Raineach (Buachaille Etive Beag)	925	
Stob Coire Leith (Aonach Eagach)	940	
Stob Coire Altruim (Buachaille Etive Mor)	941	
Am Bodach (Aonach Eagach)	943	
Stob a' Choire Odhair	945	Yes
Meall Dearg (Aonach Eagach)	953	Yes
Stob na Broige (Buachaille Etive Mor)	956	Yes
Stob Dubh (Buachaille Etive Beag)	958	Yes
Sgorr nam Fiannaidh (Aonach Eagach)	967	Yes
Ben Dubhchraig	978	Yes
Sgor na h-Ulaidh	994	Yes
Glas Bheinn Mhor	997	Yes
Sgorr Dhonuill (Beinn a' Bheithir)	1001	Yes
Beinn an Dothaidh	1004	Yes
Stob na Doire (Buachaille Etive Mor)	1011	
Stob Dearg (Buachaille Etive Mor)	1022	Yes
Sgorr Dhearg (Beinn a' Bheithir)	1024	Yes
Ben Challum	1025	Yes
Ben Oss	1029	Yes
Beinn Achaladair	1038	Yes
Stob Coir'an Albannaich	1044	Yes
Creag Mhor	1047	Yes
Stob Coire Sgreamhach	1072	Yes
Beinn Dorain	1076	Yes
Ben Starav	1078	Yes
Beinn a' Chreachain	1081	Yes
Stob Ghabhar	1090	Yes
Clach Leathad	1099	
Creise	1100	Yes
Stob coire nam Beith (Bidean nam Bian)	1107	
Meall a' Bhuiridh	1108	Yes
Stob Coire nan Lochan (Bidean nam Bian)	1115	
Ben Lui	1130	Yes
Bidean nam Bian	1150	Yes
Average Height	**1030**	
Number of peaks over 1100m	**6**	
Number of peaks over 1000m	**16**	
Number of Official Munros	**26**	

GPS Coordinates

There is no substitute for getting to know a mountain well and being able to use a map and compass, however both GPS and an altimeter watch can be fantastic navigation aids so these items are well worth considering. Unlike in the Nevis book, GPS coordinates have not been placed on the diagrams as they tend to add to clutter; instead a small selection of readings have been listed below. These should be used sparingly but may be helpful on the odd occasion.

Mountain	Location	Coordinates
Ben Lui	Summit	NN 26638 26284
	West Summit	NN 26548 26404
	Cononish Couloir	NN 26591 26594
	Central Gully	NN 26591 26318
	Forest path / Eas Daimh	NN 25383 27520
Beinn an Dothaidh	Summit	NN 33181 40862
	West Top	NN 32687 40947
	West Gully	NN 32546 40998
	Banshee	NN 32840 40883
	Coire Daingean	NN 33197 40696
	Caoineag	NN 33138 40872
Bidean nam Bian	Summit	NN 14347 54201
	West Top	NN 14130 54244
	Hourglass	NN 14131 54252
Clach Leathad	Summit	NN 24033 49310
	Big Easy	NN 24097 49260
	Col on North Ridge	NN 23914 49577
	Pig Leathad (in gully)	NN 24308 49216
	Local Hero	NN 23887 49976
	Easain Couloir	NN 24678 49066
Creise	Dragon Bowl	NN 23877 51441
	Ghlais Couloir	NN 24016 51925
	Ghlais Face (Wonderland)	NN 24047 51737
	Smaug	NN 24015 51643
	Puff	NN 23952 51581
	Slighe Bheag	NN 23758 50267
Meall a' Bhuiridh	Summit	NN 25067 50337
	Doon Ra Ba	NN 25206 50312
	Monument	NN 25345 50304
	Wagonwheel	NN 25436 50280
	932 Col	NN 24215 50057
Stob Coire nam Beith	Summit	NN 13898 54589
	An-t-sron Col	NN 13390 55003
	Massacre Face Col	NN 13895 54460
	Beith Bowl	NN 13454 54685
Stob Coire nan Lochan	Summit	NN 14839 54858
	Broad Gully	NN 14734 54944
	Forked Gully	NN 14714 55000

 skimountain

Equipment

There is a danger when writing about equipment choice in a guidebook such as this that the information will go out of date extremely quickly. At the time of writing the snowsports industry has been very active in developing products, particularly for the backcountry and touring markets, so going into too much detail here has been avoided. Having said that, the thing that will remain unchanged in this area is the nature of the terrain on offer. The skiing at White Corries is lift accessed, and here using normal downhill kit is both appropriate and good for your technique. All of the skiing elsewhere in the book, including heading over the back of Meall a' Bhuiridh towards Creise and Clach Leathad, involves varying degrees of manual effort and in these cases some sort of touring setup will probably start to become desirable.

There is a dramatic difference in weight between conventional freeride kit and lightweight touring kit. How much weight you have on your feet makes an enormous difference to how easy you will find going uphill. At the time of writing the weight differences seen between different setups is impressive. The table below is purely for illustration purposes, and where the right performance / weight / street-cred compromises sit for you depends entirely on your personal desires... the main thing is to be aware of the impact these choices can make on your skiing and your enjoyment of differing activities – get the right kit for the right day, and you'll have a blast. At the same time, keep things in perspective – as the history section shows, the right attitude goes a long way to ensuring you have a fun day out with your buddies, no matter what you have on your feet!

Some different ski setups and corresponding weights.

Setup 1	(in Kg)
Fat powder ski	2.2
Step-in touring binding	1.3
Stiff Alpine ski boot	2.3
Total for Pair	11.6

Setup 2	(in Kg)
Mid-fat freeride skis	1.8
Pin bindings (with brakes & high DIN)	0.6
'Freeride' touring boots	2
Total for Pair	8.8

Setup 3	(in Kg)
Lightweight touring skis	1.35
Pin bindings (with no brakes)	0.3
Lightweight touring boots	1.2
Total for Pair	5.7

It is worth noting that with the lightest of ski running setups it is possible to get even lighter – in some cases under 3kg is even possible. However, these uber-lightweight 'skimo' race setups are not suitable for general freeride or touring activities.

The lightweight touring boots of several years ago left much to be desired in downhill performance, but provided your pockets are deep enough it is now possible to get lightweight boots of just over a kilo each with fantastic walk modes that are nonetheless stiff enough to ski even the hardest of routes in this book. The only caveat to this is that these lightweight boots do tend to struggle as skis move into the fat and heavy category, so it makes sense to pair light with light and vice versa.

There are a number of step-in touring bindings currently on the market that offer great ease of use and downhill performance. However, this category of bindings to date seems almost immune to the need to save weight – heavy touring bindings are fine for short distances, but a very good way to make you feel unfit if you intend to go uphill with any seriousness. For this reason, young fit skiers should be encouraged whenever possible to use heavy kit to give the oldies half a chance, although intentionally blunting the edges of your kids skis and putting rocks in backpacks is perhaps a step too far.

 skimountain

A Brief History

Glencoe is the oldest ski resort in Scotland, and as such there has been plenty written about the place. So much so, that it seems unlikely that anything new will be written in these few pages, but stories thrive and live on when retold so forgive any repetition and read on. There is in fact so much history and rich folklore surrounding skiing in Glencoe that it could probably justify a book all of its own… but others are best placed to write that volume, so in the meantime a flavour is given below of some of the notable events. Although the author has tried to avoid them, please forgive the inevitable omissions and inaccuracies.

The Road to Snow

Driving through Glencoe to get to the snow these days on the A82, it is easy to forget the fact that it has only relatively recently become so accessible. At the Northern end of Glencoe, it was not until 1975 that the Ballachulish Bridge opened, and prior to that you had to either take the ferry or drive round via Kinlochleven. The road itself has a rich heritage and in many places it follows one of the old military roads that were built (by Wade's successor Major Caulfeild) in the mid-18th Century to keep the Jacobites at bay and more generally to make the Highlands a more accessible (and therefore more controllable) place. The military road was later improved by Thomas Telford in the early 19th Century as part of a massive project to improve the network in the Highlands.

The modern route of the road dates from 1932, and in many places in Glencoe you can still see the remnants of the old single track road. The improvements to the road during the mid-war years went hand in hand with a popular movement to escape the cities to the Scottish hills, with hill-walking, mountaineering, and climbing providing a backdrop to the growing awareness of the potential of the sport of skiing.

Early Skiing in Glencoe
by Jimmy Hamilton

There can be little doubt that the first person to take skis to the summit of Meall a' Bhuiridh would have been a member of the Scottish Ski Club. There is a report of an ascent, though not necessarily the first, in 1929, by Harold Mitchell: leaving his car at the highest point of the old road, his route took him up past the present Ski Club Hut and probably up ski tow gully to the summit. However, the first people to ski regularly on Meall a' Bhuiridh were members of the Creagh Dhu and Lomond Mountaineering Clubs. Founded in the early thirties these were the first working class people to take to the hills in Scotland.

Both clubs began to ski in the 1930's. Skiing was usually done when heavy falls of new snow made climbing conditions unsafe. The favoured spot in Glen Coe was on the slopes of Meall a' Bhuiridh behind Ba Cottage – a substantial, empty building on two floors which lay beside the old road. The cottage was owned by the Black Mount Estate, and provided a superb 'doss' which was used for many years with the tacit approval of the estate. A film made by Sam Drysdale of the Lomonds in that era showed that quite a number of the club were skiing, though not very skilfully by modern standards.

During World War 2, restrictions prevented the Lomond's bus from operating, but climbers from both clubs did manage to ski and climb in Glen Coe albeit on a less regular basis. The end of the war in Europe and the availability of ex-army skis and other equipment saw a new generation of young working-class climbers and hill walkers take to skiing. No one had any formal tuition, nor had anyone been to the alps; some had learned to ski in the Army while others had copied Norwegians seen in the Cairngorms. By 1947 a group of the Lomonds known as 'The Wee Crowd', had become competent if rough skiers, able to ski parallel and to do stem Christies on steep slopes. Of the Creagh Dhu, Harry McKay and Bob Clyde (who could do a Telemark) were the best. Most people at that time were still skiing in Tricouni nailed climbing boots.

The Lomonds bus still went to destinations all over Scotland, so skiing was done on Ben Lawers at Killin, at Glen Shee, at Glen Clova, and usually twice a year at Aviemore. However Glen Coe, because of the climbing possibilities, was a regular destination.

During the war years sporting activities on the Black Mount estate had been almost nil, leading to an over abundance of deer. The poaching of deer, first of all on a small scale by climbers, and latterly by more organized gangs at Ba Cottage, has been written about in Jock Nimlin's biography. The cottage was also being vandalized for firewood, and on advice from the local police it was burned down by Estate Keepers in late 1948. This was a big loss to the skiers of both clubs.

By the winter of 48/49 the Wee Crowd of the Lomonds had located a camp site on the Black Rock side of the mountain. It was on a small green sward near an old ruin some way up from Black Rock Cottage, near where the present ski patrol hut stands today. From this base they explored and skied the runs that we all know today in Corrie Pollach.

By 1950 this group of Lomonds had realized the potential of the old structure near their tent. They cleared out the debris, levelled the area and built up the fallen walls. They then walked the three miles to Ba Cottage where they recovered some partly burned beams and some sheeting and carried it back to their new site. This formed the structure of the roof, which was then covered by a heavy duty tarpaulin. The Lomond's doss, as it became known, was born.

By the early 1950's Black Rock was the established centre of skiing on Meall a' Bhuiridh, and lots of new skiers were camping in the field behind the cottage. Prominent among these were members of the Ski and Outdoor Club, known universally as 'The Socky', who began to run a bus on a regular basis to Glen Coe.

One of the early Glencoe dosses

photo **Jimmy Hamilton**

Chris Lyons built the next doss which was erected in the small quarry near Black Rock Cottage. It was a very crude structure – just some timber covered by a railway hap. This was shortly followed by something more ambitious when a group led by Frith Finlayson built a well thought out structure, partly cut into a gravel bank, which had the benefit of being very inconspicuous. Using materials donated by the county and various private companies, it even had an annexe for skis and wet gear. Used by Creagh Dhu members when climbing nearby, the doss team often gave shelter to washed out campers, and offered a friendly sanctuary in stormy weather. In 1955 the Hamiltons and Johnny McLennan also built a small doss in a secluded spot above the old road. Thus far, the building of dosses at Black Rock was accepted by the Estate.

However, when the Socky put up a large club doss just beside the main road, the Estate were stung into action and the new accommodation was immediately dismantled by the keepers, and all flammable parts burned. This doss had been largely made from indestructible steel panels and these were left strewn over the site and the wreckage was destined to become part of climbing history. For some years the Creagh Dhu had a very simple doss right below the Buachaille – an old sheep fank, some timber, and a railway hap – but with no flooring, it was damp and drafty. When well known climber and character Jimmy Jackson came home from the USA, he took a long holiday and spent much of it in Glen Coe. During this time he was the instigator and driving force leading to the remains of the Socky doss being transported to the Creagh Dhu spot below the Buachaille. There it was to be erected, re-covered, and named 'Jacksonville', first as a new climbing base for the Creagh Dhu and latterly as a Mountain Rescue Base and an iconic landmark in the climbing world.

Some of the old timers from the thirties carried on skiing until quite recently: Chris Lyons of the Creag Dhu became an influential figure in the Glencoe Ski Club; Peter McGeoch of the Lomonds was an active player in many key Glen Coe developments such as the first snow fence and the SSC Hut; Sam Drysdale remained a skier and SSC member all his life.

Sadly, the generation of skiers from the 1930's have passed away . However, a few of the next generation who began to ski in the 40's, like the Wee Crowd, are still to the fore and they have supplied this link to the past.

The section on 'Early Skiing' above was written by Jimmy Hamilton and has been published here with his kind permission – Jimmy was the designer of several early Scottish ski lifts including the Cliffhanger which is still in use at Glencoe today.

The Wee Crowd and the Big Idea

The list of names belonging to the Wee Crowd and other early Glencoe skiers reads as a who's who of Scottish Skiing: in addition to the names mentioned above, Jack Williamson from the Lomonds led the way to form the Rescue Party at Glencoe, the foundations of Ski Patrolling in Scotland (the Rescue Party / Ski Patrol at Glencoe is still manned by a strong tradition of volunteers at the weekends and many are the offspring of the founders); Bob Clyde went over to manage Cairngorm (along with Tommy Paul amongst others) and was influential in the Scottish ski industry for many years; Frith Finlayson started BASI; and last but far from least there was Philip Rankin…

Next time you have a spare few minutes at the car park at Glencoe, it is well worth reading the old SSC Journal articles that have been posted in the corridor by the toilets at the ticket office. These articles recount how a young spitfire pilot recently returned from the war, named Philip Rankin, recognised that a boring job and city life was not for him and followed a less-travelled path. From 1952 he argued eloquently for the Scottish Ski Club hut at Beinn Ghlas (erected in 1932) to re-establish itself at Meall a' Bhuiridh. In doing so, Philip showed great foresight in picking such a snow sure, North facing mountain, accessible to the cities, and with roads generally unhindered by snow closure.

Initially, there were some efforts to build a cheaper, homemade tow on Meall a' Bhuiridh, with Bill Blackwood being the main proponent. But after what must have been an epic four year struggle, and at a cost of almost £8964 (around £215k in 2014 money), the first permanent fixed ski lift was erected in the summer of 1955. The tow followed Ski Tow Gully next to the Main Basin and it opened to the public in 1956. A chairlift at Glenshee followed soon after, but it would be another eight years before there were tows at Cairngorm. Opening this first fixed tow was a pioneering act and led to an entire snowsports industry growing in Scotland that still exists and thrives today.

During the late fifties, the momentum was shifting towards development in the Cairngorms, and in 1958 the Scottish Ski Club decided to divert money away from Glencoe to focus on Cairngorm.

The first permanent Scottish ski tow

This forced Glencoe to seek alternative funding to continue their development, and the result was the formation of a new business partnership with the financial backing of the owner of Black Mount Estate, Major Fleming. This was the birth of the White Corries private company that marked the start of commercial ski operations in Scotland.

Over the next forty years, Rankin oversaw the continued development of skiing at Glencoe, with the original single-man Access Chair being built in 1959-60, followed by the Wall T-bar in 1963 (later extended in the late '60s), the Cliffhanger Chair was built in 1973, the Plateau Tow in '83, the Rannoch Button in '85, and the current two-man Access Chair and Café in 1990. For a time there was also a tow (of sorts) that was mainly used to ferry goods, materials, and employees across the plateau and was nicknamed EFFIE by Rankin to highlight its intended use (Emergencies, Freight, Fractures, and Insured Employees).

As he approaches his century, Philip Rankin continues to live in his home of Ballachulish – he retired in 1992 after 40 years but managed to go skiing at the Millennium. As has been said elsewhere, thank goodness Rankin decided to throw his bowler hat in the Clyde and go skiing instead, otherwise who knows where and if Scottish skiing would be now.

photo **Glencoe Mountain Collection**

Just some of the faces behind skiing at Glencoe, taken at the 60 year anniversary of its inception

photo **Andy Meldrum**

The Recent Past and the Latest

Rankin retired in 1992, leaving Peter Weir as General Manager for a number of years. But a combination of factors, not helped by some poor snow years, have led to many twists and turns of the ski resort's fortunes in more recent years. The resort was owned and run for a period by the same company who owned Glenshee, but a string of bad snow years left the company in financial trouble and at one point it looked like the resorts might have to close. A die-hard group of White Corries locals and volunteers persuaded Glenshee to let them open the lifts themselves during the winter of 2004. And the following summer David Campbell stepped in with a business partner to buy the resort. In 2009, the business again looked in jeopardy until Andy Meldrum and his family came up trumps and took the company on.

The future of Glencoe Mountain Resort now seems once again in good shape. There are many exciting development plans afoot and it is likely that the piste and lift map shown in this book may well need to be updated before too long. Investment is being made upgrading the infrastructure including the hill's electrics and huts. A new dry slope, more 'Hobbit Houses', an additional beginners lift, and the possibility of a new chair, will all help modernise the lift system and improve capacity. Meanwhile plans for an enormous zip line from near the top of the Access Chair are taking shape with the real hope that the future of the resort will be secure for a long time to come.

First Descents

Little emphasis has been given to listing first descents in this book – although there have no doubt been some notable ones over the years. The problem is that skiing has not had a tradition of recording descents, so it is inevitable that deeds will be missed out. Having said that, a few names are probably worth mentioning even though this will only scratch the surface of the many adventures people have had here.

In 1957 Bill Smith made full use of the new ski lift to clock up over ten thousand metres of descent - an 'Everest' in a day. Philip Rankin himself was keen on going over to Creise most springs during the '70s and '80s. Ian Watt and Iain McCluskey bagged a trip down the East Ridge of Clach Leathad in the 1980s, while the twins Bruce and Eric Thomson explored lines on the South Face of Bhuiridh, naming 'Wagonwheel' along the way. Wul Thompson skied Stob Coire nan Lochan's Forked Gully by chopper in the eighties.

As with elsewhere in Scotland, Martin Burrows-Smith was one of the early proponents of skiing the steeps and in the early to mid-eighties Martin bagged descents of Ben Lui's Central Gully, Stob Coire nam Beith's Summit Gully, Boomerang and Forked Gully on Stob Coire nan Lochan, and even a slightly surprising descent of Number 2 Gully on Aonach Dubh. George Paton and others were also skiing on Bidean from the Lost Valley in the early eighties.

There have been a number of intermingled possies of Glencoe riders in the last couple of decades who have been exploring continuously, with descents of lines on Creise, Clach Leathad, the Black Mount Traverse, Ben Lui, and many others. Danny Maddox was one well liked and strong skier amongst these assorted groups of friends, and unfortunately he was caught in an avalanche in the Cam Ghleann during 2013 – an event which rocked the Scottish skiing community. Other individual names are too numerous to mention (though some are mentioned or appear in photos elsewhere in the book) and riders travel here from right across Scotland and have frequently been unaware of what others have been doing.

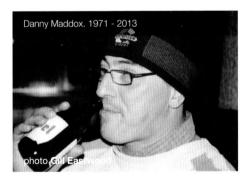
Danny Maddox. 1971 - 2013
photo Gill Eastwood

The massive amount of snow during 2014, coupled with the growing sharing of adventures and conditions on the internet, saw a surge of interest in skiing in Glencoe's mountains with numerous parties making trips to Ben Lui, Bidean and Lochan, and of course over to Creise and Clach Leathad. The majority of routes seen in this book saw descents during the 2014 season, and the pictures shown in part provide a record of that snowy season.

Exploration

This book is intended to give you a good introduction to the excellent skiing in this area, but there are plenty more inviting lines out there waiting for you to paint fresh tracks on them. So don't feel constrained to the routes described in these pages – go forth and explore! In particular, there are rich pickings for skiers venturing to the slopes of the Glen Etive hills (for example Ben Starav and its neighbours, although the sea-level start may be off-putting for some); and just beyond the reach of this guidebook on the North shores of Loch Tay are the Ben Lawers hills which not only boast some brilliant skiing and a rich skiing history, but also a high car park.

Sgor na h-Ulaidh, Beinn Fhionnlaidh, Beinn a' Chrulaiste, the slopes of Sgorr Bhan above Ballachulish, and a few others lie comfortably within the book's area but were omitted; partly because of time constraints, but also in part because of slightly trickier / longer access or lower slopes, or because the skiing seems consistently more appealing on the bigger hills close by – having said that, these hills offer excellent adventures and perhaps the fact that they have been left out of this book may even make them more appealing to some.

The hills neighbouring Ben Lui and Beinn an Dothaidh offer fantastic touring and skiing possibilities that haven't made it into this edition, and of course there are other big hills in the surrounding area such as Ben More, Ben Lomond, and Ben Cruachan that are worthy candidates for ski missions. No doubt it will not escape people too, that the long range of the Mamores lies to the North of Kinlochleven, sandwiched in between the area covered by this book and that covered by the Nevis Range and Ben Nevis volume. Likewise, a quick trip across the Corran ferry onto the Ardnamurchan peninsula (on a rare occasion when there is low-lying snow) may open the door to numerous uncharted ski adventures in amongst rugged and remote terrain.

So read the book, buy some maps, and go exploring!

Glen Etive hills and others from the top of Bidean.

photo Kenny Biggin

The author in his natural environment

photo **Neil Muir** | rider **Kenny Biggin**

About The Author

After beginning his skiing journey in the West Highland Ski Club at Glencoe in the late eighties, Kenny Biggin grew up skiing the Back Corries of Nevis Range in Scotland. In 2007 Kenny founded the SkiMountain brand as a way to build his life around his passion for skiing, and in 2013 he wrote and published the first offpiste skiing guidebook in this series. During the unprecedented snow year of 2014, Kenny returned to his roots and spent several months re-visiting and exploring the spectacular mountains of Glencoe – writing this Glencoe guidebook as a result. Whenever possible Kenny joins his Team SkiMountain buddies to seek out steeper and deeper slopes worldwide and has skied and toured in the backcountry of New Zealand, Canada, Norway, and of course the Alps. However, he still considers Fort William and the Scottish Highlands home.

Thanks for the Support

© SkiMountain